How to Win
Lotteries,
Sweepstakes,
and Contests
in the 21st Century

by
STEVE
LEDOUX
"America's Sweepstakes King"

SANTA
MONICA
PRESS

SANTA MONICA PRESS LLC
P.O. Box 1076
Santa Monica, CA 90406
1-800-784-9553
www.santamonicapress.com

Printed in the United States

Santa Monica Press books are available at special quantity discounts when purchased in bulk by corporations, organizations or groups. Please call our Special Sales department at 1-800-784-9553.

This book is intended to provide general information. The publisher, author, distributor, and copyright owner are not engaged in rendering personal finance, investment, tax, accounting, legal, or other professional advice and services, and are not liable or responsible to any person or group with respect to any loss caused or alleged to be caused by the information found in this book.

This is a revised edition of *How to Win Lotteries, Sweepstakes, and Contests.* ©1995

Library of Congress Cataloging-in-Publication Data

Ledoux, Steve, 1960-
    How to win lotteries, sweepstakes, and contests in the 21st century / by Steve Ledoux.
        p.   cm.
    Rev. ed. of: How to win lotteries, sweepstakes, and contests. c1995
    ISBN 1-891661-07-8 (pbk.)
        1. Lotteries—United States. 2. Sweepstakes—United States. 3. Contests—United States. 4. Gambling—United States. I. Ledoux, Steve, 1960-   How to win lotteries, sweepstakes, and contests. II. Title
HG6126.L43   1999
795—dc21   99-37841
                                                              CIP

Book and cover design by **cooldog**design

Contents

Millions of Dollars to be Won

YOU ARE PROBABLY FAMILIAR with the old saying, "What a difference a day makes." A more appropriate phrase today is "What a difference a century makes!" The 21st century is the most exciting and profitable time to be an active, knowledgeable participant in lotteries, sweepstakes, and contests! One thing the new millennium won't change is the same wonderful fantasy that most of us share.

How many times a day do you catch yourself dreaming about what life would be like after winning 1 or 2 or even 10 million dollars? What would you do first? Would you move to an ocean-front mansion? Travel the world? Buy a Rolls Royce for weekdays and a Porsche for weekends? Or would you, as many others have done, keep your life very much the same and invest for a secure future for your family? You might be surprised at the number of lottery winners that keep their day jobs.

But these dreams are what inspire us. They are the reasons for our hard work and dedication, and there are as many different dreams as there are people. Fantasies like these can be pleasant diversions from the daily grind. But this book isn't about fantasies or imagination. It's about helping to make your dreams come true by helping to better your odds of winning.

Each year, millions of dollars are won in sweepstakes and contests by people just like you. In spite of these millions being won, many people still simply refuse to believe that they have a chance of winning. The majority of the population continues to be skeptical about such games, feeling that you simply can't get something for nothing. These people feel as if it's not worth their time or effort to enter. They often resort to the time-worn excuse, "No one really wins anyway." But this could not be further from the truth. You can rest assured that most sweepstakes and contests are completely legitimate, there are very few incidents of fraud or cheating, and the winners are not friends of the judges. And now that you have begun to take the first step toward increasing your odds of winning, you might want to take a moment to thank those people who don't enter contests and sweepstakes. Their refusal to participate only means better odds for those of us that do!

But why does it always seem like somebody else wins? Quite simply because most people just don't have the discipline to become a winner. It's certainly not difficult, but like most endeavors, winning does take some amount of resolve and dedication. Often, people's refusal to take even the first step prevents them from going any further. Think about this. How often have you been reluctant to enter a sweepstakes or contest just because you didn't think you would win? But how can you possibly win if you don't even enter? As an old baseball player once said, "You've gotta take your turn at bat to hit a home run." The same holds true for you.

There are few guarantees in life. This book offers only a simple one: I can give you the tips that will allow you to significantly increase your chances of winning. And once you win that first prize, you'll want to win again. You will look forward to getting your mail like never before. You may decide to keep a lucky bottle of sun block around the house in case you win a cruise or a Hawaiian vacation. There are all kinds of prizes out there, just waiting to be won. It is exciting to receive valuable prizes and cash, delivered straight to your door. Imagine going on an exotic, adventurous, all-expense-paid dream vacation, or driving a brand-new car with no car payments to worry about. Add to this a long list of smaller prizes that will help make your life more enjoyable—a new pair of shoes, perhaps some good music and a nice stereo to play it on.

No matter what you may now believe, it's possible that all this is available to you simply by filling out some sweepstakes forms, entering contests, or buying lottery tickets. Once I learned how to successfully enter, the prizes began rolling in. In my first few years of successful entering, I won almost $20,000 worth of cash and prizes. And the prizes are continuing to come in. Perhaps you're like many other folks who don't consider themselves "lucky" enough to win such prizes. No problem. With my book, you'll discover the surprisingly simple methods that have helped me achieve my goal of becoming a sweepstakes winner—luck or no luck.

And you're just in time.

In the new millennium, you can bet that more and more companies are going to capitalize on the attention being paid to the 21st century. This attention will translate into contests and sweepstakes with huge, mega-sized prizes. We're already seeing the trend toward bigger prizes, and what better excuse than the new millennium to inspire companies to really dig deep into the corporate prize vault?

Additionally, with the technological advances of the last few years, there are plenty of new ways to enter sweepstakes and contests. The Internet is a perfect example of how technology has presented a wealth of opportunities for people who want to win. As advertisers and sponsors look for ways to introduce consumers to their products through web pages, the variety and volume of web-based sweepstakes and contests is increasing rapidly.

But how do you find out about and enter web-based sweepstakes and contests if you don't have a computer? That's easy. Most reputable sweepstakes newsletters provide information on these Internet opportunities, and that information should include the rules of the contests and alternate means of entry.

In the new century, we are also faced with the advantages and problems of technology. Because our personal information can be transferred in a matter of seconds between computers, we can enjoy conveniences that we were previously not able to even consider. From just about any ATM in the world, we can access our bank account information in a matter of seconds. Unfortunately, this same technology can allow our personal information to be transferred from a legitimate contest, sweepstakes, or mailing list to one with fraudulent intentions. Mailing lists are bought and sold every day in this country, and in some cases, contest and sweepstakes sponsors reserve the right to compile and even sell your personal information. Sales like these can translate into hundreds of pieces of junk mail, SPAM e-mail, and faux contests for those of us that submit our information for legitimate contests.

There are plenty of legitimate wins out there, so don't be discouraged by a few bad eggs. By the end of this book, you'll know how to spot them. You'll also know how to capitalize on the thousands of good eggs that are out there. And believe me, they're out there. It's been over 5 years since the last edition of this book, and I am still winning and enjoying the process of entering lotteries, sweepstakes, and contests more than ever! Of course every entry can't be a winner, but the possibility of winning a major jackpot, grand prize or even a smaller one is a thrilling daily prospect. Even though I enjoy other hobbies and activities, I have yet to find anything that provides the excitement, relaxation and rewards that entering to win produces.

Let me update you on some of my wins!

In 1996, I won the grand prize in a sweepstakes sponsored by KABC radio that included a chance to appear in the musical production of *Show Boat* at the Ahmanson Theatre in Los Angeles starring Cloris Leachman and Ned Beatty. Also included were tickets for 10 friends to attend both the show and a gourmet dinner at Bernard's restaurant in the Biltmore Hotel. I only entered the sweepstakes once, with a large decorated envelope. My role in the play was that of a passenger on the Cotton Blossom boat in the first scene, and before I stepped onto the stage,

Material from the Show Boat *Sweepstakes. Here I am with actor Ned Beatty, backstage before the curtain rises.*

the stage manager made an announcement to the audience that I was joining the cast for the performance. And there I was, in a costume from the 1880s, waving at the cast members on the "shore" from the bow of a mechanical boat. After my appearance, I quickly changed into my civilian clothes and joined my friends in the audience. After the play, we were all invited backstage to meet the actors and actresses and to tour the set.

In June of 1998, I won a contest sponsored by Miller Lite—a search for the biggest Dodger fan. The prize included the honor of throwing the ceremonial first pitch at a Dodger Game. To enter, I had to write a paragraph on my qualifications as the Dodger's biggest fan. My letter was chosen, and I realized that I had not thrown a baseball in years. The few days between my notification and the big game were filled with impromptu practice sessions, and when I couldn't find a friend who would sit in as catcher, I practiced by throwing at the trunk of a tree. The big day finally arrived, and I was introduced to a crowd of 38,000 over the stadium's P.A. system. As I walked out to the pitcher's mound, I could see my face on the super-sized Dodger television screen. Now that's thrilling!

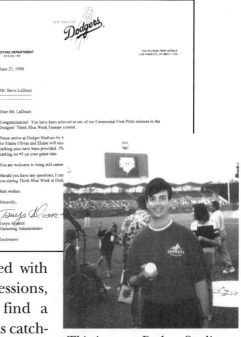

This is me at Dodger Stadium getting ready to throw out the first pitch!

My practice paid off, and I threw a strike pitch to the Dodger catcher, and despite the fact that the Dodgers were having a losing season, they won that game against the Pittsburgh Pirates!

And the vacations . . .

One of the most fascinating trips that I won was a trip to Berlin, Germany to see the Rolling Stones perform at the Coliseum. Included in the trip was roundtrip transportation, accommodations at the Hilton located in what used to be East Berlin, special

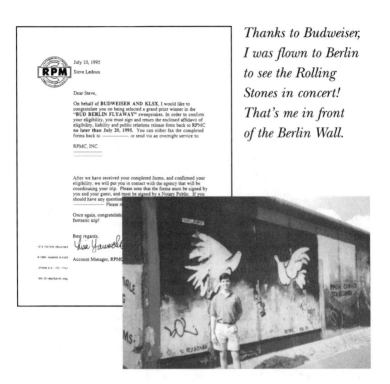

Thanks to Budweiser, I was flown to Berlin to see the Rolling Stones in concert! That's me in front of the Berlin Wall.

events, meals, tours, and the concert itself. The concert was sponsored by Budweiser beer, and I found the entry forms while shopping at my local drugstore. There was a gigantic display of Budweiser beer with an eye-catching cardboard cutout along with entry forms. I only took a few forms back home, which I quickly filled out and mailed in. I noticed that there was an alternative way of entering by calling into a radio station. As it happened, one of my entry forms was chosen, and as I took in the historic sights of Berlin and watched the Stones concert, I kept thinking to myself that all it took to get here was an entry form and a stamp! The concert was a blast, the seats were terrific, and being a part of the screaming, sold-out audience was tremendously exciting.

If you are like me, you have an idea of what your perfect vacation getaway would be. Mine has always been a cruise, and thanks to my sweepstakes hobby, I won a Caribbean Cruise on Carnival Cruise Lines. The sweepstakes was sponsored by Diet Coke, and as part of the prize, the winners appeared in a Diet Coke commercial that was filmed aboard the ship! We were filmed on camera answering

Having fun on a Caribbean cruise I won through Diet Coke.

The letter from the Los Angeles Times *informing me of my prize of a trip to Maui!*

why we love Diet Coke, and because I am a huge Diet Coke fan, I didn't have any problem answering the question. I took day excursions to the Mayan ruins of Tulum at the Yucatan Peninsula, and I was treated to a submarine ride in the Grand Caymans with spectacular views of the beautiful fish, plant life, and coral reefs.

I have won trips to Las Vegas, Catalina Island, Hawaii, and a couple of weekend getaways to San

Francisco. I also won a trip to Puerto Rico and was introduced to what have become two of my favorite pastimes—besides winning, of course—snorkeling and scuba diving.

In addition to the vacations, the last 10 years have produced the following wins:

- A year's supply of vitamins (especially valuable during the cold and flu season)
- An Olympic pin set including commemorative pins from each of the Olympic games
- A Joe Montana Upper Deck card ($250 value)
- A $500 gift certificate for patio furniture (for correctly filling out a crossword puzzle in a local newspaper)
- An Apple computer and printer
- Three color televisions
- Too many gift certificates to count
- A $2,000 guitar, with guitar lessons from a jazz master
- Rollerblades
- A bread maker
- An expensive pair of hiking boots
- Over 35 compact discs
- 80 long-distance calling cards
- Tickets, airfare, and accommodations to see a Dodger game in San Francisco
- Two fax machines
- $500 in cash
- $100 cash from Pizza Hut's *Celebrity Delivery Second Chance Sweepstakes*
- $100 in free video rentals
- A Sony Car Discman
- Four tickets to Disneyland
- A ski trip for two to Lake Tahoe

- A Weber Grill and Harry and David steaks
- A case of shampoo
- Tickets to the zoo
- A skateboard
- A *101 Dalmatians* dog food bowl and a dental cleaning for April, my West Highland terrier!

My desire to win began years ago with game shows. Before I even realized the opportunities that were available in the world of sweepstakes, contests, and lotteries, I'd already had great success as a game show contestant. Over the last several years I've racked up wins on shows including *Match Game, Hot Streak, Blackout,* and *Quicksilver.* (You may never have heard of a few of these games, but that's good; I'll tell you why later on.) I considered making a career out of being a contestant, but I soon learned that there are rules that restrict the number of game shows on which a person can be a contestant, but more about that later. My game show victories got me hooked on winning.

I then turned my attention toward the countless other sweepstakes and contests that are out there—ripe for the picking. And, as I soon discovered, there's no limit to the number of such contests you can win. You'll learn a little later in the book just how many opportunities are out there, and how to track them down.

But I got off to a rather shaky start. Without any guidance or knowledge about the world of sweepstakes and contests, I relied solely on luck. Don't get me wrong, good fortune is a wonderful thing, but in terms of sweepstaking, it's not the most important thing. After several years of misguided effort, I came away with a couple of tacky key chains and ugly T-shirts. I ended up being so discouraged that I gave it up.

Still, that excitement of winning cash on the game shows lingered. And since I wasn't allowed back on a game show for several more years, I took another run at sweepstakes. But this time I did my homework. Through trial and error, through experimentation and hard work, I came up with a plan. It's the very same plan contained in this book. And then I put my plan into action.

My first windfall came while shopping at a well-known grocery store chain. As it happened, the store was promoting its 25th anniversary with a sweepstakes. Using a few of the tricks I'd learned, I entered the contest at each of the chain's 12 stores. Guess what? I won a trip to Puerto Rico—the chain's grand prize. I also won three color televisions from three individual stores. And I won a gift certificate worth $100. It was clear that my system was working pretty well. I was off and running.

A few weeks later, I rounded the corner of an aisle in another grocery store and almost knocked over a display for a Diet Coke giveaway. A cruise to the Caribbean sounded pretty good, so I entered. Three weeks later, I got the good news that my techniques had worked again. My dreams of winning had come true. Other trips quickly followed—San Francisco, Las Vegas, to name a few—so many that I decided to stop entering such contests for the

The lucky letter with news of my grand prize win of a trip to Puerto Rico!

time being. Because of work, I just didn't have the time to take all the trips I knew I could win! Nor did I want to pay the taxes on prizes that I would not be using.

To give you an example of how well my plans were working, I decided to enter a cooking contest. This is something akin to Attila the Hun becoming a teacher at a charm school. No matter. Despite my lack of cooking talent, I knew what the judges would want. And when I gave it to them—a recipe I called "Cracklin' Double-Nut Fried Chicken"—I received a $300 first prize and a fancy certificate suitable for framing.

Now my friends, family, and co-workers ask me for advice on sweepstakes. "What did you win today?" has become a common refrain around the office. People think that I'm the luckiest person on Earth. But while luck may indeed have something to do with my success, you don't really need it to win.

Winning isn't the only positive result of my success. One of the most rewarding aspects of my hobby is being able to share my experiences and advice with others. In addition to this book, I have conducted several seminars in major cities across the United States. These seminars give me an opportunity to share my experiences with others, and more importantly, they offer the audience a chance to meet others who share their enthusiasm for winning.

I usually begin each seminar by asking each person in the audience their reason for attending. What I have found is that the majority of the attendees are really only interested in strategies for winning large lotteries. What they don't realize is that by limiting themselves to only lotteries, they are missing out on sweepstakes, contests, and game shows that offer much better odds than lotteries alone.

Why are most people interested only in the lottery? There are a few reasons. Lotteries are typically run by state governments, and people have faith that the process is fair and just. Also, most people have heard about illegitimate sweepstakes, scam contests, and slick phone solicitations that have taken innocent people for a lot of money. You'll learn tips for spotting phony sweepstakes and contests a little later in the book. The final reason, perhaps, is that, in general, lotteries represent the créme de la créme of winnings. The sheer amount of money involved makes lotteries the ultimate fantasy.

One exercise that I always perform at the seminar is to have the attendees list three prizes that they would

Poster from 1969, the first contest I ever won!

really like to win. I also ask them to write down three ways they would spend the money if they were to win a lottery. I have found that it helps to visualize yourself winning the prize. It may not necessarily increase your odds, but visualization allows you to have a more positive attitude throughout the entry process. Also, if you really visualize the prizes you want to win, you are more likely to focus on those contests that will help you reach your goals.

These seminars have allowed me to meet interesting people from different parts of the country, and their willingness to learn more and their desire to win inspires everyone around them, including me.

CHAPTER 1

Lotteries, Sweepstakes, and Contests

— AN OVERVIEW

ALTHOUGH YOU MAY BE NEW to lotteries, sweepstakes, and contests, rest assured they go back thousands and thousands of years. It seems that right after mankind invented money, he invented games of chance to win. The word "lot" (as in lottery) dates back to the time of the Old Testament, where it was used to describe an object that's used in a game of chance. The Lord even told Moses to divide land among Israelites "by lot." The ancient Romans and Egyptians also used lots for gaming, as did the Greeks.

By the sixteenth century, something familiar to the lottery we know today had already developed in

Europe. Queen Elizabeth was such a fan of the lottery (and the money it put into her bank account) that she started a lottery in England in 1566. Even our own forefathers in colonial America authorized lotteries to help build churches, schools, and bridges. Not only are lotteries as old as civilization but they also occur in every corner of the globe. There are lotteries in Africa, South America, and several Asian countries. And as democracy begins to flourish in Eastern Europe, more and more lotteries have begun there as well.

Alexander Hamilton's feelings about the lottery still hold true today, even for contests and sweepstakes: "Everybody, almost, can and will be willing to hazard a trifling sum for the chance of considerable gain." That's what this book is about: taking a small chance with the hope of winning amazing benefits.

A Relaxing Hobby

Before continuing with the idea of winning prizes—the main point of this book—let's quickly return to the attitude you should take as a lottery, sweepstakes, and contest entrant. Once again, you should think of it as a hobby. Sure, it may be difficult at times to separate yourself from your fantasies. There's nothing wrong with that. Entering lotteries, sweepstakes, and contests, like any other hobby, is something to be enjoyed in your free time. You should relish the tension of waiting until the winners are announced. Go right ahead and fantasize about the day when you become a winner, quit your job, and move to a tropical island. You should dream of sitting down behind the wheel of that Ferrari you always wanted. I myself would buy a 50-foot sailboat with as many accessories as I could think of and head straight to Bora Bora. A friend of mind wants nothing more than to open his own hardware store in a pretty mountain town and sell nuts and bolts to the locals. What's your dream?

I believe that entering sweepstakes and contests has been widely overlooked as a means of unwinding from the stresses and strains of everyday life. I find that sitting down in front of the television after a long day at the office, and taking a little time to fill out entry forms, decorate envelopes, and think of new ways of winning can be quite therapeutic. You should enjoy the process of entering sweepstakes and contests and not just its rewards. If you can do that, then you'll never be a loser. Your life will be enriched by spending your free time doing something you find truly entertaining.

Being a lottery, sweepstakes, and contest entrant is much like watching sporting events on TV: While we often hope for a certain outcome, most of the joy actually comes from simply watching the event. Of course, some people are even able to turn their hobby into a profession, winning so many sweepstakes and contests that they can quit their regular jobs and devote all their time to entering such promotions. These folks are able to win with surprising consistency, earning houses, cars, money, and other prizes. The IRS, realizing that sweepstaking can be a considerable source of extra cash, now recognizes prize winnings as a legitimate source of income.

The Right Attitude

Now let's return to the rewards. The prizes are there to be won, and they are sometimes more exciting, exotic, and expensive than you would ever dare imagine. Italian sports cars, custom-built houses, millions of dollars in cash, and many other prizes are regularly given away in lotteries, sweepstakes, and contests. While it is impossible to guarantee that you can become a winner, you can significantly increase your chances by following the suggestions outlined in this book.

My first two suggestions both have to do with attitude.

By now you already know what the first one is: Don't be afraid to enter, and enter as often as possible. Don't allow yourself to be overcome by fears of losing. Even the regular winners lose more frequently than they win, and sometimes the most you have to lose is the price of postage. Keep reminding yourself that people really do win—and win every day across the country.

Take Pam Hiatt, for example. In 1995, Pam was a Boise State University student, unmarried, pregnant, holding down two part-time jobs, and desperately hoping to scrape together enough money to rent a small studio apartment. On June 3, 1995, she stopped at Jackson's Food Store for a breakfast of orange juice and a doughnut. She bought a multistate Powerball ticket as well and, the next morning, discovered that she had won over $87 million dollars. She had played the ages of her family members and, to show her appreciation, bought each one of them a new car. Needless to say, she didn't have any problems affording a place to live, and in spite of winning around $3.1 million a year for the next 20 years, she did not choose to live in a mansion. After appearing on David Letterman, Pam settled down in a modest, three-bedroom house. Her future plans include starting a charitable foundation for foster kids, and to continue to do her own cleaning and yard work.

Or how about Deborah Cook? Deborah was a stressed-out working mother of three who, on a whim, decided to enter a Maybelline Beauty Cruise contest. After scouring local stores for entry forms, Deborah took the time to fill out 60 entries over the next 3 weeks. Her husband thought she was crazy until she won a week-long cruise. It was their first vacation away from the kids since their honeymoon. As Roger Tyndall, a legendary sweepstaker once said, the key to winning boils down to the three Ps: Persistence, Patience, and Postage.

The second suggestion is to do your homework. Many people never achieve the level of excellence they desire in their hobbies because they don't seem willing to put the necessary time into it. If gardening is your hobby, you will need to study the different types of plants and what type of care each needs. If your hobby is working on cars, then at some point you will probably need to read up on mechanics. My point is, all hobbies take time, and entering sweepstakes and contests is no exception. By doing your homework, I mean that you should take the time to learn the rules of different sweepstakes and contests. Are you allowed to enter more than once? Is any purchase necessary? Should you type or print the entry form? In fact, it is estimated that at least 25 percent to perhaps as many as 50 percent of all sweepstakes and contest entries are thrown out because the entrants don't follow the rules. Let's think about that . . . one quarter to one half of all entries are thrown out! Now how do you feel about your odds? Are the rules that stringent? No, but if you don't read the rules closely, you may miss some little tidbit. Wouldn't it be horrible to know that the entries you spent three hours putting together were thrown out because you didn't include a phone number? So read those rules, and just think of how great your chances are increased.

Lotteries and Sweepstakes versus Contests

You're probably aware of the words "lotteries," "sweepstakes," and "contests," but you may not really understand how they differ from one another. This section will discuss their differences, as well as their relative advantages and disadvantages.

It's easier to define sweepstakes and contests by starting with their more familiar grandfather: the lottery. A lottery is any game that consists of three elements. These three elements are chance (luck), the entry fee (sometimes referred to as the "consideration"), and the prize. The first element—that of luck—is introduced by the very fact that you're competing against thousands of other people by predicting several numbers that will be chosen at random. The entry fee is generally the price of the ticket itself. Most lottery tickets cost one dollar. And the prizes are usually money.

What differentiates a sweepstakes or contest from a lottery is that one of the three elements has been removed. In a sweepstakes, that element is the entry fee. In other words, the game is still a game of chance, and there are still prizes to be won (although not necessarily cash prizes), but you don't have to pay to enter.

Contests, on the other hand, retain the element of the entry fee but remove luck as a determining factor. The entry fee is usually in the form of purchasing one or more of a company's products. For example, a contest often requires you to send in a proof of purchase or label. Obviously, you cannot obtain these items without buying the product. It doesn't matter whether you personally bought it or if one of your friends purchased it. The luck is removed by adding a requirement of skill. Whereas sweepstakes are determined through random drawings, contests require the participants to perform in some way. A contest may ask you to write a song or create a rhyme, or even explain why you use a product. A panel of judges then determines which contestant they feel has demonstrated the most skill.

People tend to believe that contests are more legitimate simply because they're sometimes required to pay an entry fee. One reason that companies like contests so much is that it is another way of generating very affordable advertising. Not only does the contest itself increase consumer interest, but the company might even end up with a catchy slogan or jingle for their product when the contest is over. This slogan might be just as good as one created by a professional marketing firm, and the prize they give to the winner is likely to be less expensive than the cost of hiring such a firm.

How to Spot Phony Lotteries, Sweepstakes, and Contests

A word of caution is due at this point. Although most sweepstakes and contests are legitimate and legal, illegal versions of them do exist. Never participate in any illegal sweepstakes or contests, as there is no guarantee that you can ever collect your winnings, or even that the sweepstakes or contest has any winners at all. Illegal sweepstakes and contests are also fundamentally wrong, and law enforcement agencies spend millions of dollars every year trying to put an end to them. So don't make their job more difficult than it already is.

Often a "scam" win will appear out of the blue. In other words, you will receive a confirmation for a contest or sweepstakes that you have not entered, or one that targets citizens "at random." A good rule of thumb is that if you haven't officially entered a contest or sweepstakes and a company notifies you that you have won, be very careful and investigate each "offer."

One of the newest, and most prevalent contest scams is the spread of 900-number "contests" that promise big prizes but almost always deliver nothing more than huge phone bills. You may have already received something in the mail that promises you've won a prize—a Ferrari, a color TV, a gold chain. Included in the package is a 900 number that you must call to collect what you've won. Trouble is, it might cost you $30 or $40 in phone charges to find out that you've won a gold chain worth 2 or 3 bucks. I once received what looked like a check for $7,500 made out to my name. A letter accompanying the check stated that my name had been entered in a national sweepstakes, the cash was due to me, and I was going to receive a bank check for up to $7,500. The letter also instructed me to call the company's 900 number as soon as possible to give my security code check ID number.

Now, before I tell you the obvious evidence of a scam, let's look at what I knew so far. First, it is a rarity to receive a check for a large sum of money in the mail. Is the check cashable at your bank? Of course not. Second, the letter stated that my name was entered in a national sweepstakes. This was vague language, and I knew that I didn't enter my name, which meant it was probably chosen at random. Two red flags, one more to go. Third, I knew that 900 numbers cost money to call, and legitimate sweepstakes do not require this. As I suspected, there was more to the letter. They went on to inform me that the call cost $3.98 per minute, and an average call was 6 minutes long. Also, on the back of the check in small print, were the odds of winning. I could squint to see that my odds in winning the $7,500 were actually 1 in 4,998,468. However, the odds of winning $1 were 1 in 1. So, let's do the math. If I called the number, I was guaranteed to win one dollar. I was also practically guaranteed to spend almost four dollars. However, if my call was as long as the average call, I would spend almost $25! For the odds of winning $7,500, I might as well take the money and buy 25 lottery tickets. The odds aren't that much worse, and the prize is much bigger.

There are also numerous phone "contests," such as spelling and sports trivia, which promise a big prize for answering a number of questions. In one such contest, callers pay $2.99 a minute to try and spell 21 words. You have to spell all the words correctly to win, and they don't tell you if you've misspelled any words until you've tried all 21. A ten-minute call costs $30, and chances are good you'll lose. While legislation is being enacted to ban such scams, many are still operating legally throughout the country. My advice is to stay away from any and all "900" contests and giveaways.

Vacation scams are another popular way of cheating people out of their money and time. I received a very official-looking certificate stating that I had been selected for a fantastic vacation package for two. The form included a reservation number for a tropical vacation package for seven days and six nights aboard a cruise ship. I called immediately, and found out that there were fees associated with the package that amounted to hundreds of dollars and no airfare was included. Conveniently, the company was a full-service agency, and I could purchase the airfare through their service. The cheerful operator told me to be sure to pack my sunscreen and forget about any diet I might be on, as the buffets on the cruise were world-renowned. She then added, with a giggle, to make sure and send her a postcard. I must admit, she was very effective in making me feel like I had actually won something, and someone not acquainted with legitimate contests might easily be taken advantage of by such an effective salesperson, which is exactly what she was.

After telling her that I travel to exciting locations several times a year as a result of winning legitimate sweepstakes, and that these sweepstakes did not require me to pay for anything, her delightful tone quickly changed. She mumbled a quick goodbye and moved on to another victim. Beware of those "winnings" that conceal hidden costs or require you to purchase something to collect your prizes. Some popular vacation scams often involve you sitting through lengthy, high-pressure sales pitches for time-shares on vacation homes. While this may not seem unreasonable to some, the sales pitches often consume so much of your vacation time that you have very little left over to actually enjoy yourself. Other scams promise "dream vacations" and deliver only substandard accommodations.

I once went to an office to pick up what I thought was a trip to Hawaii. But instead of getting a free vacation, I sat through a dull sales pitch for condominium time-shares. The very least they could have done was to send me to Hawaii and give me the sales pitch on the island. And, as I hope you already know, no legitimate contest or sweepstakes will ever require you to give a credit card or bank account number.

Lotteries are almost always legitimate, but you must remember that they are only legal when run by governments at the state level. No other government, private corporation, or individual may hold a lottery in this country. So if you run into one that is not orchestrated by a state government, then you are advised to steer clear of it and perhaps even report it to the police. It is unlikely that you will ever encounter an individual, corporation, or government holding an illegal lottery, as such events usually garner huge amounts of attention and publicity, but confidence tricksters have been known to attempt virtually any scam they could conjure up.

One of these scams is the Foreign Lottery. You may have received some sort of promotional material in the mail that advertises a big return on investments in foreign lotteries. Companies will also use telemarketing to get to you. What you should know is that these foreign lotteries are illegal. Additionally, they are almost always scams perpetrated by a fraudulent American company and are not even sanctioned by the government of the country being used in the sales pitch. You should also know that even purchasing foreign lottery tickets is illegal in this country. And even if you were to ignore the legality issue, another big showstopper comes next. How do you guarantee that the company will invest your money in a foreign lottery? Do you know what the lottery tickets in other countries look like? Not that you will ever see one from the "investment" company. If you receive any mailings of this nature, the best thing you can do is send the entire package to your local Better Business Bureau.

Here are some general tips for avoiding fraud:

- If you are required to pay money in order to win something or collect a prize, the caller is a fraud.
- If you don't remember entering the sweepstakes or contest that you are being confirmed as having won, it is not a legitimate win.
- Legitimate sweepstakes do not require credit card numbers, money, or additional personal information to award a prize.
- Do not make purchases over the telephone.
- If you are contacted by a company either by mail or over the phone, do not take immediate action. Get the person's number and extension, along with the name of the company, and tell them that you will call back at a better time. Do not commit to anything, and do not give out any personal information. This serves two purposes. It prevents you from immediately falling for a convincing sales pitch and gives you some time to think about what is being offered. Secondly, it allows you some time to call your local Better Business Bureau and check the company out. However,

fraudulent companies are in the business of deceiving people, and just because the Better Business Bureau does not have information on a specific company does not necessarily mean that the company is on the up and up. Companies that are reported often "go out of business" and reopen some time later under a different name.

Try to use your best judgment when dealing with possible scams. Report any suspicious activity as soon as possible, so you can help prevent others from being taken advantage of.

One truly important legal matter to be aware of is that some states are very strict as to what types of sweepstakes and contests they will allow—we've all heard the phrase "void where prohibited by law." Many people have actually been lucky winners in the past but were never able to collect their winnings simply because the state in which they lived had previously disallowed the sweepstakes or contest. Occasionally, these states still sometimes refuse to allow sweepstakes and contests (also known as "promotions") within their borders because of the horrible corruption that surrounded them at one time.

Until the early 1900s, individuals were actually allowed to hold lotteries, but no one ever seemed to win them. Corporations promised even bigger prizes than they do now, but none were ever awarded (and participants were forced to buy products, even though they shouldn't have been). As a result, laws governing promotions became very strict, and some states are still wary of them. So if you live in one of the few states where certain types of promotions are prohibited, then try not to be bitter about it. The people who made the laws had your best interests in mind, and they weren't trying to stop you from having fun.

How can you find out if a sweepstakes or contest you would like to enter is illegal in your state? Chances are, if you received the promotion in the mail, then you probably live in a state where it is legal. At one time, corporations that held sweepstakes and contests would send out their mailings indiscriminately, but this resulted in some fairly lengthy legal battles with several state that did not allow certain promotions. Rather than go through that again, many corporations now simply avoid sending some of their mailings to these states.

But even if you do receive the mailings, this does not automatically mean that promotions are legal in your state. First try checking the rules on the promotion; these should clearly indicate which states prohibit such a promotion.

If you are truly concerned that a particular sweepstakes or contest might be illegal in your state, you could try writing a letter to a member of your state government. Legislators' addresses can always be found in your local phone book, and if you happen to write to one who doesn't know whether or not a certain promotion is legal in your state, then he or she will surely pass on your letter to someone who does know.

Now that you are aware of certain basic features of promotions, we're ready to move on to helping you choose which type of lottery, sweepstakes, or contest is best for you. The following sections of the book will go into various promotions in great depth, including the strategies that may help you become a winner. Maybe one day we'll meet on a cruise to Tahiti!

CHAPTER 2
Lotteries:
A Ticket
to Wealth

I'LL SAY IT AGAIN SO you'll get the message: People win lotteries every day across this country. Keep that in mind the next time you hear about how long the odds are. Think about Andy Davidson of Evansville, Indiana, who bought his winning ticket at the Junior Food Mart in Henderson, Kentucky, while buying gasoline. He wasn't worried about the odds, and on June 18, 1997, Andy won $57,569,536.47.

Ever since 1964, when New Hampshire became the first modern state lottery, Americans have been lining up for a chance at the elusive pot of gold that lucky people like Andy Davidson have found. The lottery craze sweeping the nation is fueled, in large part, by the government's need for more funds. Just a few decades ago, the idea of state-run gambling (which is really what lotteries are) would have been out of the question. However, as I am writing this book, there are only three states that do not have state lotteries: Tennessee, Hawaii, and Utah. The other 47 have at least a state lottery, and most now allow other forms of gambling. Why has almost every state jumped on the gambling bandwagon? Because gambling, whether state-run or not, produces a lot of revenue. Just look at Las Vegas. The enormous amount of growth that Las Vegas has experienced in the last few decades can be directly attributed to the colossal amount of revenue generated by the gambling of millions of visitors a year.

So why are there still groups opposed to lotteries? That's a bit complicated. Some argue that lotteries and gambling attract those who can least afford to lose the money. Compulsive gambling—lotteries included—is an addiction, and some states are not willing to sacrifice the well-being of their populous for any amount of money.

However, recent studies may disprove the myth that lotteries take advantage of lower-income families. In the fall of 1997, *The Washington Post* commissioned a poll to find out who consistently plays the lottery. The results showed that middle-income households played the lottery more often than any other group. Households with incomes of $45,000 to $65,000 are more likely to play than any other income group. Can you guess which groups played the least often? The wealthiest and the poorest Americans proved least likely to spend any amount of money on the lottery, regardless of the jackpot. Those households that earn less than $25,000 almost never played the lottery, and most households with an income over $65,000 a year rarely played.

And here's something to keep in mind when you decide to play or not. How many people do you think win at the lottery every week? Twenty? Thirty? Wrong. How about 20 million? That's right. Twenty million Americans win prizes every week across the country. Obviously, they don't all win the jackpot. Most win five dollars, some win a thousand. But the point is that it's possible to win extra money without having to battle the enormous odds.

Where does the money from lottery ticket sales go? In most states, roughly 30 percent goes to a public service of some kind, usually education. Another portion is earmarked to run the lottery itself, including publicity, operating costs, and salaries. Vendors usually get about five cents for every dollar spent on lottery tickets in their store. And, of course, the remainder goes to the lucky few who hit the right combination of numbers. Most state-run lotteries will tell you where the money goes. This information is usually published in some sort of medium, and if you call or write your state lottery office, they will usually send you the information free of charge.

As you can see, the lottery craze has spread like wildfire across the country. But do lottery players really know what's involved? Do they know how much and how often they should bet or what happens to their money after they buy their tickets? Do they pick numbers at random, or do they play the same numbers every week? Do they know that they might increase their chance of winning by playing games out of state, or how one group of investors almost ensured winning a Virginia lottery? Yes, I know, the odds are slim (as slim as 14 million to one in some states). But people win every day.

In the following pages, we're going to be looking at the different kinds of lottery games that are out there and how people have increased the odds in their favor. We'll also discuss how people go about picking numbers, which is where the fun comes in.

A Variety of Ways to Win Lotteries

Lottery games don't vary much from state to state. There are basically three different types of games that are common across the country: Lotto, instant scratch cards, and various daily number games.

The big daddies, of course, are the lotto games that feature jackpots topping $100 million. It has become common for such games, which go by names such as Mass Millions, Megabucks, Powerball, and Lot-O-Bucks, to feature jackpots of $10, $20, even $30 million on a regular basis. Most lottery states require players to pick 6 numbers, usually ranging from 1 to 36, up to around 1 through 54. Obviously, the lotteries with fewer numbers to choose from have much better odds. But that also means that the prizes will be that much smaller.

On the other hand, when players have to pick 6 numbers out of 54, as in some state lotteries, it's common for weeks to go by without a winner. You've probably noticed that when a few weeks pass without a winner, the prizes start to swell. If a month or so goes by without a big winner, then the prizes become astronomical. Consider The Lucky 13, which is what a group of 13 machine-shop workers in Ohio are calling themselves after winning the world's largest lottery jackpot of $161,496,959.30 on July 29, 1998. The men held the sole winning Powerball ticket for the draw, which one member purchased in Richmond, Indiana. Each of the 13 men contributed $10 for tickets and one of the quick picks paid off.

And then there was the 1989 Pennsylvania jackpot that topped $115 million. As Damon Runyon used to say, "That's a lotta lettuce."

While we're on the subject, people often ask why state lotteries don't make the prizes smaller so that more people can win. Why have a lottery where one or two people split $100 million, when a 100 people could win a million dollars? Such logic makes sense, but think about it for a minute. Are you more likely to buy lottery tickets when the prize is $1 or $2 million, or when it's $35 million? Studies show that the bigger the prize, the more tickets get sold. And the more tickets that get sold, the more money floods into state coffers, which is the whole reason for the lottery anyway. Lottery officials love it when a jackpot gets up into the stratosphere—it insures not only big ticket sales but big publicity, which can increase ticket sales even after the big winner has been picked.

Choosing Your Numbers

But back to playing the lotto. Players have two options for picking their six numbers. Their first choice is to have a computer pick their numbers for them at random, often known as a quick pick game, since there's no fuss with filling out forms. The attendant at the store simply punches the appropriate number on the store's lottery terminal and the player is instantly assigned as many sets of six numbers as they want. Although having a computer choose your numbers for you may not be as exciting as choosing your own, statistics indicate that your chances of winning may be better if you use the computer's numbers.

Players can also choose their own numbers by filling out small forms at the store that sells tickets. (I'll talk later about the various ways people pick numbers). After the player has filled out the form, the numbers are fed into the store's lottery terminal. The numbers are then sent over telephone lines to the central lottery computer. That main computer then assigns a serial number to the ticket with the player's chosen numbers and instantaneously sends it back to the vendor with authorization to sell the ticket. Such a system ensures that you won't be shortchanged if your ticket comes up a winner. By the way, it also ensures that you won't be able to tamper with the ticket to create your own winner. Don't laugh; people try it all the time.

Winning numbers are drawn either once or several times a week, depending on the state. Even in this computer age, the selection of winning numbers is not much more sophisticated than two hundred years ago. Sure there are automated draw machines that use computer technology to pick numbers, but in most states, a rotating drum full of balls with numbers on them is spun. Then the balls are randomly released. They roll down into a slot, one by one, until six balls lay in a row. Those are the winning numbers for that drawing. Simple, right? The trick, of course, is getting the right numbers.

In the event you win (or when you win, if you're an optimist like me), the jackpot will almost always be paid in yearly installments over 20 years. I'm often asked why states don't pay off lotto prizes all at once instead of over 20 years. The answer is simple: Were they to pay every lottery winner the full amount of the prize, the state would quickly run out of money. Instead, the state invests a set amount (referred to as an "annuity") that, over the span of 20 years, will pay out the full amount of your win. Sure, money now is always better than money later. But are you really going to complain about it if you win?

You may have noticed, too, that many states have instituted minimum prizes. That way, ticket buyers can be assured of a hefty lotto jackpot regardless of the amount of tickets sold for that period. In California, for example, the minimum prize for the twice-weekly lotto is $4 million. Such minimum prizes have done wonders for ticket sales.

Keep in mind, too, that you don't have to have all six numbers to win. Picking five of the six can mean a pay-out of over $2,000 in some states. Four out of six can pay for 40 or 50 more lottery tickets. And three out of six will usually pay for the ticket you just bought, so you don't lose anything.

Daily Numbers

Most states also offer a daily game that consists of the player picking three or four numbers, usually in the same order they are later drawn. Obviously, the odds for such games are much better than with lottos, and thus the prizes are correspondingly smaller— from $500 to $5,000 depending on the game and state. It's great to increase the odds in your favor by playing daily numbers games, but it has one big disadvantage: It's just not as fun to fantasize about winning two or three grand as it is to dream about winning $2 or $3 million. Still, I highly recommend playing such games, along with the lottery, to greatly improve your chances of becoming a winner. It's always best to play the games with good odds. I try to make it a point to play these games almost every time I play the lottery.

Multistate Lotteries

The Multistate Lottery Association is owned and operated by the participating states, and the profits obtained by the individual states are retained by those states. States that participate are: Arizona, Connecticut, Washington, DC, Delaware, Indiana, Idaho, Iowa, Kansas, Kentucky, Louisiana, Minnesota, Missouri, Montana, Nebraska, New Hampshire, New Mexico, Oregon, Rhode Island, South Dakota, Wisconsin, and West Virginia.

Powerball is perhaps the most popular type of multistate lottery, but it is by no means the only game in town. The official multistate lottery site describes Powerball as an "on-line lottery," but don't let the term on-line fool you. You can't actually play over the World Wide Web. You must still purchase tickets at a lottery vendor. The six Powerball numbers are drawn from two sets of numbers. Five white balls are drawn from one set of numbers (1–49). One red power ball is draw from a second set of numbers (1–42). If you want the computer to randomly select the numbers for you, select the Quick Pick option.

At the Powerball web page, you can register to receive e-mail notification of the Powerball numbers on the morning after the drawing. You can also access a list of past winning numbers, find out more about other games offered by the multistate lottery, and check television stations and times for drawings. They even have a section where you can find out about past games. One of the great things about Powerball is that the odds of winning something are better than a standard lottery, and the jackpots are bigger. Why? The odds are better because for every ticket, there are nine different ways to win. How, you ask?

If you match five white balls in any order and the red Powerball, you win the jackpot, or grand prize. If you match only the five white balls, you win $100,000. If you match 4 white balls and the power-ball, you win $5,000, and without the powerball, 4 white matches will win $100, and so on. Matching one powerball earns you $3, and the overall odds of winning something are 1 in 35.

You can subscribe to Powerball, although the rules for subscribing vary from state to state. The individual states only allow subscriptions as an options for residents of the state; you cannot sub-scribe if you do not live in a sponsor state. Therefore, you must either buy the ticket in person or subscribe, and if you do not live in a state that sponsors Powerball, you must travel to the nearest state that does to purchase a ticket. Also, like most state lotteries, you can either take a lump sum payment or annual payments, which are made over 25 years. You must make the choice at the time of ticket purchase.

Winning Powerball tickets are valid for 180 days. You must redeem your multistate prize in the state where you bought the ticket.

The drawing location changes occasionally, but the times are always the same: 10:59 p.m. Eastern time every Wednesday and Saturday night.

For more information about multistate games, visit the multistate lottery web site at www.musl.com or write the Multistate Lottery Association at:

Multistate Lottery Association
1701 48th Street, #210
West Des Moines, IA 50266-6723
(515) 453-1400

Wild Card

The multistate *Wild Card* game is currently available in Idaho, Montana, and South Dakota. With Wild Card, you pay one dollar and get two plays. For each of the 2 plays, you pick 5 numbers between 1 and 31, and 1 from 16 different Wild Cards. As with most state lotteries, you also have the option to let the computer select the numbers and wild card for you. Wild Card drawings are held every Wednesday and Saturday night.

The multistate lottery commission draws five numbers out of 31 and a Wild Card from a deck of 16 face cards. You can win cash prizes by matching three, four, or five numbers. If you also match the Wild Card, your prizes get even bigger. And every Wild Card match is a winner. Compared to traditional lotteries, the odds are much better. In fact, the overall odds of winning some prize by playing Wild Card are about 1 in 6.

Cash 4 Life

Cash 4 Life is a new multistate game sold in Washington DC, Indiana, Iowa, Kansas, Minnesota, Montana, Nebraska, New Hampshire, South Dakota, West Virginia, and Wisconsin. The Cash 4 Life grand prize pays $1,000 per week to the winner for the rest of his or her life, with a 10-year minimum payout.

Each $1 ticket contains 15 sets of numbers, and at the time of the drawing, four balls are drawn out of a drum of 100 balls marked 00-99. If you match all four numbers in the Lifetime Grand Prize group, you win the grand prize. You can also win cash prizes of $100,000, $50,000, $25,000, $20, and $1 by matching numbers in other groups. And for those of you that are worried about having to share $1,000 a week, the chances of that are slim. The Lifetime Grand Prize is not split among the winners unless there are more than three winners in a day.

Instant Games

The instant lottery games have become increasingly popular in recent years. Although not as much of a cash cow as the lotto games, such games have been quite lucrative for states. The scratch-off cards that can be purchased in most grocery stores come in a variety of forms, from poker games to slots to sporting events. One state even issued a scratch card to commemorate a state anniversary.

In general, the small cards (which usually cost a dollar) have a series of six latex-covered circles. When scratched off, they reveal the prize, or lack thereof. For example, with a poker-style game, revealing three face cards might win $10 or more. Revealing a royal flush might be the big winner.

Such cards offer the pleasure of instant gratification: You buy it, you take a nickel or a quarter and scratch, and you know right away if you've won or not. There's no waiting around for drawings. The only problem, of course, is the stuff that falls onto your lap when you're scratching the card. A San Francisco columnist calls it "lott moss," which is as good a name for it as any.

Of all the lottery games, the scratch cards offer the best odds of winning a few bucks; most states have instant games that feature winning tickets out of each six or seven cards. And while prizes rarely exceed $25,000, most states have scratch cards that offer a chance at a larger prize if you have the winning combination. In California, for example, a card that has three "big spin" emblems under the latex covering will get you onto a Saturday night drawing on live television. Most states use a spinning wheel of fortune for such drawings, which can be quite dramatic as participants wait for the ball to drop into the slot that determines whether they'll win 10 grand or a cool million. One of the more memorable winners of a $2 million prize was a nun, who probably had a bit of help from above. As you might imagine, the scratch games are produced under stringent security, utilizing computer manufacturing. The winning cards are distributed randomly within bundles of five hundred tickets. Officials from the lottery act as inspectors, often randomly choosing a ticket to check its security code against computer records. As with the big lottos, by checking these codes on each card, dealers and lottery officials can insure that the card is an actual winner and not, as sometimes happens, a forgery. The security is equally stringent at the drawings where the $2 million prizes are awarded.

CHAPTER 3

How to Increase Your Odds of Winning Lotteries

LET ME BEGIN THIS CHAPTER by repeating a joke I heard recently. Stop me if you've heard it. A man named Ed goes into church one bright Sunday morning and, looking up, whispers, "God, help me win the lottery. I've got to win the lottery!" He repeats his prayer the following week and every week for the next month. Finally, after he's left church one Sunday and is watering his lawn, a voice booms down from the heavens: "EDDDD!" the voice says. "Do you think you could help me out a bit by actually buying a ticket?!"

The joke illustrates the most basic and important principle of playing the lottery: You have to buy a ticket to win—even with heavenly intervention on your side. That's just one of the helpful hints we'll be discussing in this chapter on how to help bend the odds back in your direction. Although such hints don't insure a jackpot (do you think I'd be here writing this book if I'd won a $20 million jackpot?), they do help increase the odds. And they might also make the game more enjoyable, which I think is the most important aspect of any kind of lottery, sweepstakes, or contest. Let's get to it.

HINT I: You've gotta play to win.

As God told Ed, this is the first rule in lotteries, sweepstakes, and contests. It's doubtful that anyone's going to buy you a ticket without your knowledge, so get out there and do it yourself. But I'd recommend against pushing your luck—don't do what the disheveled, elderly gentleman who walked into an Illinois liquor store holding a paper bag full of cash did. He bought $10,000 worth of lotto tickets, but recouped only a few small prizes from his investment— an outlay he obviously could not really afford to make. Another man in Florida dumped $80,000—his life savings, as it turned out—into a big Florida lottery, only to walk away a loser as well. These two examples illustrate one of the unflinching truths about lotteries: You can buy enough tickets to increase your odds to 1 in 2, but that still leaves 50 percent to chance.

It is true that increasing the amount of tickets you buy will increase the odds. The Florida man, for example, changed his odds from 1 in nearly 14 million to 1 in 175. That's not as overwhelming as one in 14 million, but you still stand an awfully good chance of walking away empty-handed, which he did. By playing just $10, he would have improved his odds a bit and not had the awful anxiety that must have accompanied his bet.

How often should you play? It depends on whether you play a certain set of numbers every time you play or just grab a quick pick now and again. I myself have been playing the same numbers for eight years. It's too late for me to switch. Besides, it's only two dollars a week. By the way, you can buy your tickets in advance (more on this later) so you don't have to run to the store twice a week to get them. If you just like to play the quick pick (which I do, as well), then get tickets whenever the mood strikes, or whenever the jackpot gets your fantasies stirred up.

So my rule of thumb on this is simple: You've got to play to win, but play within your means. This may sound like a no-brainer to some of you, but it is not uncommon for people to develop addictions to gambling, and the lottery is a form of gambling.

With that in mind, I like to keep track of my lottery winnings and losses. I do this for several reasons. One, it gives me a clear picture of which games seem to be paying off and which don't. It also keeps my losses in check and gives me a succinct record at tax time. If I find, for example, that I've spent $400 in the last nine months, I might want to cut down on my spending. As in all things, moderation is key.

HINT 2: Don't play numbers that other people are likely to pick or numbers that form a pattern on the lottery ticket.

Can you imagine what it would be like to beat the incredible odds against you and actually win a lottery, only to find that thousands of other people have the same numbers and your prize is only worth a few thousand dollars?

Sound impossible? It's not.

As you probably know, lottery winnings fall under the classification of "pari-mutuel." That means that, like many horse races, each winner receives a portion of the jackpot divided equally among all the winners. If you're the only winner, you walk away with the whole pot. If five people win, you win one-fifth, and so on. Obviously, you want to maximize the amount you win by being the only one with the correct lottery numbers.

It won't surprise you that most of the numbers picked by players are between one and 31. Why? You guessed it—that's how many days of the month there are, and many people pick birth dates as lottery numbers. Filling out a form using only numbers up to 31 increases the odds that someone else will have the same numbers, and that you'll have to split the jackpot. Likewise, many lottery players consider the number "7" as lucky. Thus many lottery tickets have the numbers 7-14-21-28-35-42—all multiples of seven. If such numbers come in, you might have to split the pot with a few hundred other players.

Nor should you try to fill out your lottery form in such a way as to create some kind of pattern, like an "X" or "Y." Trust me, lots of people have the same idea. And on at least one occasion, the pattern, in this case a 'V,' did indeed yield a winner. Problem was, 74 players had the exact same pattern. What should have been the greatest moment of their lives turned out to be one of the most disappointing. Each walked away from the lottery grand prize with a measly four grand. That's better than nothing, but it won't buy a Ferrari.

The loud-and-clear message here is that if you're going to choose your own numbers, make sure they're unique. Otherwise, you may be setting yourself up for a big letdown.

HINT 3: Play the computer's numbers.

I hate to admit it, but those quick pick games have resulted in dramatically more winners than any of the so-called "systems" that lottery experts have come up with. As you've seen, I'm a big fan of picking my own numbers, but more for the fun of it than because of any statistical advantage that might come my way. The evidence is rather overwhelming that a simple quick pick ticket is up to six times more likely to be a winner than its handpicked counterpart. Besides the better odds, you are also much less likely to have to share your good fortune with another winner, since it's extremely unlikely that anyone else will have a quick pick number. But it has happened, as you'll see later on in the book. So if you don't get any enjoyment from picking numbers, then play the quick pick.

HINT 4: Play lottery games that increase the odds in your favor or increase the prize money—even if it means paying a little more for the ticket.

More and more states have initiated games that give the player the chance to better the odds, usually for the nominal fee of one dollar. Oregon (a state that is often on the cutting edge of lottery games) has something they call the "Kicker," which makes smaller wins much more attractive by quadrupling the prize for a measly dollar for every buck you bet. Let's say you get a ticket that has 4 out of the 6 numbers, and let's say the usual prize for such a win is around $40. If you paid for the Kicker option, your increased cash prize would be around $160. This is a bargain that just can't be overlooked. Check with your state lottery to see if such a game is offered. If it is, by all means take it.

HINT 5: Check your tickets for winning numbers right away.

In Michigan several years ago, a $10.5 million prize went unclaimed, so the money was funneled back into lottery coffers. It's interesting to speculate about the fate of the winner. Did they stick their ticket in a mayonnaise jar and forget about it? Did they become ill or pass away before the winner was announced?

I don't want that to happen to you. So my advice is to read the paper the very next day to see if you've won or not, or even watch the lottery broadcast in your state to know immediately. For most lottery players, this isn't really an issue. The sheer excitement of a big jackpot is enough to send them to their televisions or newspapers as soon as the numbers are made public. But there are enough well-publicized examples to warrant me mentioning it. And, by the way, you should always keep your tickets in a safe, dry place. It would be a shame to have your dog eat a $10 million winner. And remember if you have access to a computer and the world wide web, a quick way to check lottery results is to log onto a site that posts winning numbers.

HINT 6: There's no such thing as a "hot" or "cold" number. Don't bother with them.

I've talked to many people who subscribe to lottery tip sheets or 900-numbers that feature lottery numbers that seem to be occurring with regularity. While it's true that you may notice certain numbers appearing frequently, you shouldn't let that fact determine the numbers you pick. Let me explain why. The main thing you need to know is that lottery numbers occur randomly. That means that you simply cannot predict what the next number will be.

Let's say you're rolling a die over and over again. Although some numbers may seem to come up more times than others, if you kept rolling the die more and more times, you'd find that each of the six numbers will come up just about the same amount of times. That's over the very long haul, not over 10 or 20 rolls. The same is true for lottery numbers. Unless you're truly psychic (in which case you've probably already won several lotteries), you just can't predict the next set of numbers based on a few numbers in the recent past.

The same holds true for numbers that have not occurred in recent lottery games. A lot of people play these so-called "cold" numbers in the misguided belief that they'll show up in the next few games. While it's true that those numbers will eventually show up over the long haul, it could be weeks, months, or even years. Remember, lottery numbers occur randomly. It is, to coin a phrase, a crapshoot. As I just mentioned, stick with quick pick games, which is about as random as you can get.

HINT 7: Join a reputable lottery pool near you.

While it's always best to win the big jackpot by yourself, you should still do everything you can possibly do to increase the odds in your favor. I've found no better method than to join with a group of honest people in a lottery pool.

You may already have such a pool at the office, but in case you don't, let me explain how it works: In general, a lottery pool is any number of people who band together to buy a larger number of lottery tickets than they could individually afford. They also agree to split the winnings equally. For example, a lottery group with 20 members might each chip in $5 a week, giving the group a total of 100 lottery tickets per week. Each individual in the group has increased the odds of winning by twenty-fold. And while the jackpot might not be as large, in these days of mega-lotteries, splitting a prize 20 ways could still leave you a millionaire. Remember, too, that you'll also greatly increase your chances of winning smaller prizes, which could mean thousands of dollars in your pocket.

Although there are different types of lottery clubs, most seem to originate at the workplace. I recommend these over most other types, mainly because of the built-in trust involved, as well as the convenience of having all the players in the same proximity. In general, duties such as collecting money from the players, buying the tickets, and making Xerox copies of the tickets for each of the players are simple. You might even want to form your own club. I believe that if you want to play the lottery with any seriousness, you should be in a lottery club. If you have any doubts, just monitor lottery wins in your area; you'll see that more and more of them are won by the happy members of lottery pools.

However, beware of lottery syndicates!

We need to differentiate here between the small, friendly pools that are proliferating across the country and the massive lottery syndicates that try to buy literally every possible ticket. That's right—every ticket. You may have read of the famous 1992 case in which a syndicate from Australia invested $5 million in the Virginia lottery in an attempt to insure winning the $27 million jackpot. They were attempting to buy every possible permutation—$7 million in all—of the 6-number game. They would have succeeded, too, had they had enough time. It didn't matter, though. Their 5 million tickets contained the winner.

In order to win, they had to fill out 5 million lottery forms and monopolize hundreds of lottery machines across the state in a race to beat the deadline. They were very lucky. There were still 2 million numbers that could have come up as the winner, leaving them $5 million in the hole. Besides that, some lucky Virginian, or several lucky Virginians, could have come up with the winning number as well, splitting the jackpot down to a prize with less than $5 million. But things worked out, and the Australian syndicate made more than a five-fold return on their investment. Although it was all perfectly legal, many states have enacted rules to prohibit such chicanery. Many players were outraged at having to wait in line behind a syndicate employee who was buying thousands and thousands of tickets.

My advice to you is to stay away from joining any such syndicate. There's a very good chance you'll lose your money. And, while the return could be good if you win, you'll have to invest quite a bit to make it worth your while.

HINT 8: Some states have special promotions whereby they allow you to mail in losing scratcher cards that give you a chance to enter million-dollar drawings.

In case you doubt this, just remember the California woman who was chosen for the scratcher drawing not once but three times, earning her over a million bucks. Check with your local state lottery office to see if they are currently running such a promotion. Here are the addresses and phone numbers of state lottery offices:

Arizona State Lottery
4740 E. University Drive
Phoenix, AZ 85034
(602) 921-4400

California State Lottery
  Headquarters
P.O. Box 3028
Sacramento, CA 95814
(916) 323-7095

Colorado State Lottery
P.O. Box 7
Pueblo, CO 81002
(719) 546-2400

Connecticut State
  Lottery
Russell Road
P.O. Box 11424
Newington, CT 06111
(203) 566-2912

Delaware State Lottery
  Office
The Blue Hen Mall
Suite 202
Dover, DE 19901
(302) 739-5291

District of Columbia
  Lottery Board
2101 Martin Luther
King Ave. S.E.
5th Floor
Washington, DC 20020
(202) 433-8000

Florida State Lottery
  Headquarters
Capitol Complex
250 Marriott Dr.
Tallahassee, FL 32399
(904) 487-7777

Georgia Lottery
  Corporation
250 Williams Street
INFORUM, Suite 3000
Atlanta, GA 30303
(800) GALUCKY

Idaho Lottery
P.O. Box 6537
Boise, ID 83707
(208) 334-2600

Illinois State Lottery
201 E. Madison
Springfield, IL 62702
(217) 524-5155

Indiana
The Hoosier Lottery
P.O. Box 6124
Indianapolis, IN 46206
(317) 264-4800

Iowa State Lottery
2015 Grand Avenue
Des Moines, IA 50312
(515) 281-7900

Kansas State Lottery
128 N. Kansas
Topeka, KS 66603
(785) 296-5700

Kentucky Lottery
1011 West Main Street
Louisville, KY 40202
(502) 560-1500

Louisiana Lottery
11200 Industriplex
Suite 150–190
Baton Rouge, LA 70809
(504) 297-2000

Maine State Lottery
  Commission
10-12 Water St.
Hallowell, ME 04347-1431
(207) 287-3721

The Maryland State
Lottery
6776 Reiserstown Rd.,
Suite 204
Baltimore, MD 21215
(410) 318-6200

Massachusetts State
Lottery Commission
15 Rockdale Street
Braintree, MA 02184
(617) 849-5555

Michigan Bureau of
State Lottery
P.O. Box 30023
Lansing, MI 48909
(517) 335-5600

Minnesota State Lottery
2645 Longlake Road
Roseville, MN 55113
(651) 635-8100

Missouri State Lottery
1823 Southridge Drive
Jefferson City, MO 65109
(573) 751-4050

Montana State Lottery
2525 N. Montana
Helena, MT 59601
(406) 444-5825

Nebraska Lottery
P.O. Box 98901
Lincoln, Nebraska
68509-8901
(402) 471-6100

New Hampshire
Sweepstakes Commission
P.O. Box 1217
Concord, NH 03302
(603) 271-3391

New Jersey Lottery
One Lawrence Park
Complex
CN041
Trenton, NJ 08625
(609) 599-5800

New York State Lottery
Swan Street Bldg.
1 Empire State Plaza
Albany, NY 12223
(518) 457-0440 or
(518) 388-3415

Ohio State Lottery
615 West Superior Avenue
Cleveland, OH 44113
(216) 787-3200

Oneida
First American Games
P.O. Box 365
Oneida, WI 54155-0365
(800) 236-8532

Oregon Lottery
  Headquarters
P.O. Box 12649
Salem, OR 97309
(503) 540-1000

Pennsylvania State
  Lottery
Department of Revenue
2850 Turnpike
Industrial Drive
Middletown, PA 17057
(717) 986-4699

Rhode Island Lottery
1425 Pontiac Avenue
Cranston, RI 02920
(401) 463-6500

South Dakota Lottery
207 E. Capitol, Suite 200
Pierre, SD 57501
(605) 773-5770

Texas Lottery Commission
Post Office Box 16630
Austin, Texas 78761-6630
(512) 344-5000

Vermont Lottery
  Commission
P.O. Box 420
Route 14
South Barre, VT 05670
(802) 479-5686

Virginia State Lottery
P.O. Box 4689
Richmond, VA 23220
(804) 786-0000

Washington State
  Lottery
814 4th Avenue
Olympia, WA 98506
(360) 753-1412

West Virginia Lottery
P.O. Box 2067
Charleston, WV 25327
(800) 982-2274

Wisconsin Lottery
P.O. Box 8941
Madison, WI 53708
(608) 266-7777

One of the rewards of the Internet is that most states with lotteries have created their own web pages. These pages contain lottery results, odds, past winners, and descriptions of that state's current games. There are other sites that are not affiliated with the states that also compile state lottery information, and if you're trying to find general information on a number of state lotteries, you might visit one of these sites rather than look at the state sites individually. For lists of lottery web sites, simply visit a search engine such as Yahoo or Lycos (some Internet service providers such as AOL now have searches from their home page) and search on "lottery results," or "lotteries." Or if you want to look at the individual state types, type the name of the state followed by the word "state" followed by the word "lottery." For instance, if you wanted to find the official Texas lottery site, you would search on "Texas State lottery."

HINT 9: Don't be afraid to play in states with bigger jackpots or better odds.

Although there are, as I mentioned earlier, only three basic types of lottery games throughout the country, the odds and prizes vary dramatically. Since you should always play the lottery with two aims in mind—to increase the odds in your favor, and to win the biggest possible jackpot—you should search for games that will help you accomplish this, no matter what state. Let's say, for example, that you're choosing between games in state X and state Y. State X has a 6-39 game, where the player has to play 6 out of a possible 39 numbers. State Y requires players to pick 6 out of 53 numbers. Clearly, state X has the better odds.

But, as you might suspect, state Y has a bigger population and, thus, a much bigger jackpot. Which do you play, better odds or bigger jackpot? Here's my advice: Always go for the game with the better odds. The reason is obvious: You stand a better chance of winning.

I travel a great deal, so I always check the odds of states I'm visiting in case I get a chance to play the lottery. You should do the same. Here's an idea of what you can expect from the different states. With only a few exceptions, these are the lottery games by state, and the list contains the number of picks for each game, the type of payment method, and the odds of winning the grand prize on a one dollar play. Of course, games do change, so always check with the individual state lottery office for current information.

Arizona

Arizona Fantasy 5
Picks: 5 out of 35
Payout: Cash
Odds of $1 play:
  324,632:1

Arizona Lotto
Picks: 6 out of 42
Payout: Annuity or Cash
Odds of $1 play:
  5,245,786:1

California

California Daily 3
Picks: 3 out of 10
Payout: Cash
Odds of $1 play: 1,000:1

California Daily Decco
Picks: 4 out of 13
Payout: Cash
Odds of $1 play:
  28,561:1

California Fantasy 5
Picks: 5 out of 39
Payout: Cash
Odds of $1 play:
  575,575:1

California Lotto
Picks: 6 out of 51
Payout: Annuity
Odds of $1 play:
  18,009,460:1

Colorado
Colorado Lotto
Picks: 6 out of 42
Payout: Annuity or Cash
Odds of $1 play:
 5,245,786:1

Multistate
Powerball Lotto
Picks: 5 out of 49 (the
 red Powerball is 1 out
 of 42)
Payout: Annuity or Cash
 payout
Odds of $1 play:
 80,089,128:1

Tri-State
Tri-State 5 card
Picks: 5 out of 31
Payout: Cash
Odds of $1 play:
 3,838,380:1

Tri-State Daily
Picks: 3 out of 10
Payout: Cash
Odds of $1 play: 1,000:1

Tri-State Megabucks
Picks: 6 out of 40
Payout: Annuity
Odds of $1 play:
 3,838,380:1

Tri-State Play 4
Picks: 4 out of 10
Payout: Cash
Odds of $1 play:
 10,000:1

Connecticut
Connecticut Cash 5
Picks: 5 out of 35
Payout: Cash
Odds of $1 play:
 324,632:1

Connecticut Daily
Picks: 3 out of 10
Payout: Cash
Odds of $1 play: 1,000:1

Connecticut Lotto
Picks: 6 out of 44
Payout: Annuity
Odds of $1 play:
 7,059,052:1

Connecticut Play 4
Picks: 4 out of 10
Payout: Cash
Odds of $1 play:
 10,000:1

Delaware
Delaware Lotto
Picks: 6 out of 36
Payout: Cash
Odds of $1 play:
 973,986:1

Delaware Midday 3
Picks: 3 out of 10
Payout: Cash
Odds of $1 play: 1,000:1

Delaware Midday 4
Picks: 4 out of 10
Payout: Cash
Odds of $1 play:
  10,000:1

Delaware Play 3
Picks: 3 out of 10
Payout: Cash
Odds of $1 play: 1,000:1

Delaware Play 4
Picks: 4 out of 10
Payout: Cash
Odds of $1 play:
  10,000:1

Florida
Florida Cash 3
Picks: 3 out of 10
Payout: Cash
Odds of $1 play: 1,000:1

Florida Fantasy 5
Picks: 5 out of 26
Payout: Cash
Odds of $1 play:
  65,780:1

Florida Lotto
Picks: 6 out of 49
Payout: Annuity
Odds of $1 play:
  13,983,816:1

Florida Play 4
Picks: 4 out of 10
Payout: Cash
Odds of $1 play:
  10,000:1

Georgia
Georgia Cash 3
Picks: 3 out of 10
Payout: Cash
Odds of $1 play: 1,000:1

Georgia Fantasy 5
Picks: 5 out of 35
Payout: Cash
Odds of $1 play:
  324,632:1

Georgia Lotto
Picks: 6 out of 46
Payout: Annuity
Odds of $1 play:
  9,366,819:1

Idaho
Idaho FAST 5
Picks: 5 out of 32
Payout: cash

Illinois

Illinois Daily
Picks: 3 out of 10
Payout: Cash
Odds of $1 play: 1,000:1

Illinois Little Lotto
Picks: 5 out of 30
Payout: Cash
Odds of $1 play:
  142,506:1

Illinois Lotto
Picks: 6 out of 50
Payout: Lump Sum
Odds of $1 play:
  12,913,583:1

Illinois Midday 3
Picks: 3 out of 10
Payout: Cash
Odds of $1 play: 1,000:1

Illinois Midday 4
Picks: 4 out of 10
Payout: Cash
Odds of $1 play:
  10,000:1

Illinois Pick 4
Picks: 4 out of 10
Payout: Cash
Odds of $1 play:
  10,000:1

Indiana

Indiana Daily 3
Picks: 3 out of 10
Payout: Cash
Odds of $1 play: 1,000:1

Indiana Daily 4
Picks: 4 out of 10
Payout: Cash
Odds of $1 play:
  10,000:1

Indiana Lotto
Picks: 6 out of 48
Payout: Annuity or Cash
Odds of $1 play:
  12,271,512:1

Indiana Lucky 5
Picks: 5 out of 36
Payout: Cash
Odds of $1 play:
  188,496:1

Iowa

Iowa Cash Game
Picks: 5 out of 35
Payout: Cash
Odds of $1 play:
  324,632:1

Iowa Supercash
Picks: 6 out of 42
Payout: Cash
Odds of $1 play:
  2,622,893:1

Kansas

Kansas Lotto
Picks: 6 out of 33
Payout: Cash
Odds of $1 play:
  553,784:1

Kansas Pick 3
Picks: 3 out of 10
Payout: Cash
Odds of $1 play: 1,000:1

Kentucky

Kentucky Cash 5
Picks: 5 out of 35
Payout: Cash
Odds of $1 play:
  324,632:1

Kentucky Lotto
Picks: 6 out of 42
Payout: Annuity or Cash
Odds of $1 play:
  5,245,786:1

Kentucky Pick 3
Picks: 3 out of 10
Payout: Cash
Odds of $1 play: 1,000:1

Kentucky Pick 4
Picks: 4 out of 10
Payout: Cash
Odds of $1 Play: 10,000:1

Louisiana

Louisiana Easy 5
Picks: 5 out of 26
Payout: Cash
Odds of $1 play:
  65,780:1

Louisiana Lotto
Picks: 6 out of 44
Payout: Cash
Odds of $1 play:
  7,059,052:1

Louisiana Pick 3
Picks: 3 out of 10
Payout: Cash
Odds of $1 play: 1,000:1

Maine

Tri-State 5 Card
Picks: 5 out of 31
Payout: Cash
Odds of $1 Play:
  3,838,380:1

Tri-State Daily
Picks: 3 out of 10
Payout: Cash
Odds of $1 Play: 1,000:1

Tri-State Megabucks
Picks: 6 out of 10
Payout: Annuity
Odds of $1 Play:
  3,838,380:1

Tri-State Play 4
Picks: 4 out of 10
Payout: Cash
Odds of $1 Play: 10,000:1

Maryland
Maryland Daily 3
Picks: 3 out of 10
Payout: Cash
Odds of $1 play: 1,000:1

Maryland Lotto
Picks: 6 out of 49
Payout: Annuity
Odds of $1 play:
  6,991,908:1

Maryland Match 5
Picks: 5 out of 39
Payout: Cash
Odds of $1 play:
  575,757:1

Maryland Midday 3
Picks: 3 out of 10
Payout: Cash
Odds of $1 play: 1,000:1

Maryland Midday 4
Picks: 4 out of 10
Payout: Cash
Odds of $1 play:
  10,000:1

Maryland Pick 4
Picks: 4 out of 10
Payout: Cash
Odds of $1 play:
  10,000:1

Massachusetts
Massachusetts Daily
Picks: 4 out of 10
Payout: Cash
Odds of $1 play:
  10,000:1

Massachusetts Mass Cash
Picks: 5 out of 35
Payout: Cash
Odds of $1 play:
  324,632:1

Massachusetts Mass
  Millions
Picks: 6 out of 49
Payout: Annuity
Odds of $1 play:
  13,983,816:1

Massachusetts
  Megabucks
Picks: 6 out of 42
Payout: Annuity
Odds of $1 play:
  5,245,786:1

Michigan
Michigan Cash 5
Picks: 5 out of 39
Payout: Cash
Odds of $1 play: 575,757:1

Michigan Daily 3
Picks: 3 out of 10
Payout: Cash
Odds of $1 play: 1,000:1

Michigan Daily 4
Picks: 4 out of 10
Payout: Cash
Odds of $1 play: 10,000:1

Michigan Lotto
Picks: 6 out of 49
Payout: Annuity or Cash
  option
Odds of $1 play:
  13,983,813:1

Minnesota
Minnesota Daily 3
Picks: 3 out of 10
Payout: Cash
Odds of $1 play: 1,000:1

Minnesota Gopher 5
Picks: 5 out of 39
Payout: Cash
Odds of $1 play:
  575,757:1

Missouri
Missouri Lotto
Picks: 6 out of 49
Payout: Annuity or Cash
Odds of $1 play:
  3,529,526:1

Missouri ShowMe
Picks: 5 out of 30
Payout: Cash
Odds of $1 play:
  142,506:1

Montana
Montana Lotto
Picks: 5 out of 37
Payout: Cash
Odds of $1 play:
  217,949:1

New Hampshire
New Hampshire Lotto
Picks: 6 out of 36
Payout: Cash
Odds of $1 play:
  1,947,792:1

Nebraska
Nebraska Pick 5
Picks: 5 out of 30
Payout: Annuity
Odds of $1 play:
  142,506:1

New Jersey
New Jersey Cash 5
Picks: 5 out of 38
Payout: Cash
Odds of $1 play:
501,942:1

New Jersey Kicker
Picks: 5 out of 10
Payout: Cash
Odds of $1 play:
100.000:1:1

New Jersey Pick 3
Picks: 3 out of 10
Payout: Cash
Odds of $1 play: 1,000:1

New Jersey Pick 4
Picks: 4 out of 10
Payout: Cash
Odds of $1 play: 10,000:1

New Jersey Pick 6
Picks: 6 out of 46
Payout: Annuity
Odds of $1 play:
9,366,819:1

New York
New York Daily
Picks: 3 out of 10
Payout: Cash
Odds of $1 play: 1,000:1

New York Lotto 54
Picks: 6 out of 54
Payout: Annuity
Odds of $1 play:
25,827,165:1

New York Pick 10
Picks: 20 out of 80

New York Take 5
Picks: 5 out of 39
Payout: Cash
Odds of $1 play:
575,757:1

New York Win 4
Picks: 4 out of 10
Payout: Cash
Odds of $1 play:
10,000:1

Ohio
Ohio Buckeye 5
Picks: 5 out of 37
Payout: Cash
Odds of $1 play:
435,897:1

Ohio Kicker
Picks: 6 out of 10
Payout: Cash
Odds of $1 play:
1,000,000:1

Ohio Lotto
Picks: 6 out of 47
Payout: Annuity or Cash
Odds of $1 play:
  10,737,573:1

Ohio Pick 3
Picks: 3 out of 10
Payout: Cash
Odds of $1 play: 1,000:1

Ohio Pick 4
Picks: 4 out of 10
Payout: Cash
Odds of $1 play: 10,000:1

Oregon
Oregon Daily 4
Picks: 4 out of 10
Payout: Cash
Odds of $1 play: 10,000:1

Oregon Megabucks
Picks: 6 out of 44
Payout: Annuity or Cash
Odds of $1 play:
  3,529,526:1

Pennsylvania
Pennsylvania Big 4
Picks: 4 out of 10
Payout: Cash
Odds of $1 play: 10,000:1

Pennsylvania Cash 5
Picks: 5 out of 39
Payout: Cash
Odds of $1 play: 575,757:1

Pennsylvania Daily
Picks: 3 out of 10
Payout: Cash
Odds of $1 play: 1,000:1

Pennsylvania Wild Card
Picks: 6 out of 48
Payout: Annuity
Odds of $1 play:
  6,135,756:1

Rhode Island
Rhode Island Daily
Picks: 4 out of 10
Payout: Cash
Odds of $1 play: 10,000:1

Rhode Island Rhody Cash
Picks: 5 out of 30
Payout: Annuity or Cash
Odds of $1 play:
  142,506:1

South Dakota
South Dakota Cash
Picks: 5 out of 35
Payout: Cash
Odds of $1 play:
  324,632:1

Texas
Lotto Texas
Picks: 6 out of 50
Odds of $1 play:
  15,890,700:1

Texas Cash 5
Picks: 5 out of 39
Payout: Cash
Odds of $1 play:
  575,757:1

Virginia
Virginia Cash 5
Picks: 5 out of 34
Payout: Cash
Odds of $1 play:
  278,256:1

Virginia Kicker
Picks: 6 out of 10
Payout: cash
Odds of $1 play: 100:1

Virginia Lotto
Picks: 6 out of 44
Payout: Annuity
Odds of $1 play:
  7,059,052:1

Virginia Midday 3
Picks: 3 out of 10
Payout: Cash
Odds of $1 play: 1,000:1

Virginia Midday 4
Picks: 4 out of 10
Payout: Cash
Odds of $1 play:
  10,000:1

Virginia Pick 3
Picks: 3 out of 10
Payout: Cash
Odds of $1 play: 1,000:1

Virginia Pick 4
Picks: 4 out of 10
Payout: Cash
Odds of $1 play:
  10,000:1

Washington
Washington Daily
Picks: 3 out of 10
Payout: Cash
Odds of $1 play: 1,000:1

Washington Keno
Picks: 20 out of 80
Drawing Time: 6:59 pm
Advance Drawings: Yes; 7

Washington Lotto
Picks: 6 out of 49
Payout: Annuity
Odds of $1 play:
  6,991,908:1

Washington Quinto
Picks: 5 out of 52
Drawing Time: 6:59 pm
Advance Drawings: Yes; 5

Washington, DC
Washington, DC, Daily
Picks: 3 out of 9
Payout: Cash
Odds of $1 play: 1,000:1

Washington, DC, DC-4
Picks: 4 out of 9
Payout: Cash
Odds of $1 play: 10,000:1

Washington, DC, Midday 3
Picks: 3 out of 9
Payout: Cash
Odds of $1 play: 1,000:1

Washington, DC, Midday 4
Picks: 4 out of 9
Payout: Cash
Odds of $1 play: 10,000:1

Washington, DC, Quick
 Cash
Picks: 6 out of 39
Payout: Cash
Odds of $1 play:
 1,087,541:1

West Virginia
West Virginia Cash 25
Picks: 6 out of 25
Payout: Cash
Odds of $1 play:
 177,100:1

West Virginia Daily 3
Picks: 3 out of 10
Payout: Cash
Odds of $1 play: 1,000:1

West Virginia Daily 4
Picks: 4 out of 10
Payout: Cash
Odds of $1 play: 10,000:1

Wisconsin
Wisconsin Megabucks
Picks: 6 out of 49
Payout: Annuity
Odds of $1 play:
 6,991,908:1

Wisconsin Money 4
Picks: 4 out of 10
Payout: Cash
Odds of $1 play: 10,000:1

Wisconsin Pick 3
Picks: 3 out of 10
Payout: Cash
Odds of $1 play: 1,000:1

Wisconsin Supercash
Picks: 6 out of 36
Payout: Cash
Odds of $1 play: 973,896:1

Clearly, the pot for the West Virginia lottery is not going to be anywhere near the size of the Oregon game. Still, if I had the choice between the two games, I'd pick West Virginia. I like winning, and I'm not greedy.

With that said, however, if the games are closely matched in terms of the odds, always go for the bigger pot. As we've discussed, sometimes, after several weeks without a winner, the pot will become enormous in a state with relatively good odds for winning. I like to calculate the states with the best odds-to-jackpot ratio and, if the opportunity presents itself, play those games.

A word of warning: It is against U.S. postal regulations to send lottery tickets and any other lottery-related material through the U.S. mail. So how do you get out-of-state tickets? If you're like many lottery players across the country, you may have, on occasion, asked a friend in another state to purchase tickets for you in their home state. This is a very risky proposition. There have been numerous occasions in which a "friend" who has been asked to buy a lottery ticket decides that the winning ticket actually belongs to them, even though it began as a favor for a buddy from out of state. Unless you trust the person with your life, I'd advise against having them buy tickets. If you do have them buy tickets for you, make sure they tell you the quick pick numbers before the drawing. And, if you've picked your own numbers, make sure to check whether you've won or not. Sadly, many friendships have disintegrated, and many lawsuits filed, over just such arrangements.

The best advice I can give, especially to those on the East Coast, where a neighboring state may be close by, is to just get the tickets yourself. Most states now offer advance play, so you can actually buy tickets for lotteries months in advance. If you only get to a state with a big lottery infrequently, this affords you the opportunity to get all the tickets you want without having to make weekly trips.

If this option is impractical, there are also businesses that specialize in brokering out-of-state lottery tickets. You'll pay steeply for their services, usually about $10 for every $5 worth of tickets you order. Since the tickets are shipped to you using a private postal service, it's all completely legal. Most businesses such as these are efficient and above board, but there have been cases of both ineptitude and outright fraud. If you're considering using subscription services, be careful to check with your local Better Business Bureau to make sure the company has a good record.

HINT 10: Don't limit yourself to just lotto. Play a variety of your state's games to increase the odds.

Although it's tantalizing to carry around a potential $10 million winner in your pocket, don't forget that there are other games out there that can make you a millionaire, or at least a "thousander." Barring that, they can at least help you come out a winner. I like to get the most bang I can for my lottery buck by playing my state's "pick-3" game, as well as an occasional scratcher or two. I know that by doing this, I've increased the odds dramatically over just playing the lottery. I also try to take advantage of special games that offer more numbers for less money. Washington, DC, for example, features a 6–39 game that offers three plays for just one dollar. Many states have similar features. You should take advantage of them because they help increase your odds of becoming a winner.

HINT 11: Don't throw out those old tickets. They may come in handy around tax time.

Don't throw away those losing lottery tickets and scratchers that pile up in a shoe box, because they can still be worth money to you later on. Although your total lottery losses for the year are not deductible, you are allowed to claim them against any lottery winnings you may have. Let me try to clarify that a bit. Let's say you've spent a total of $200 last year on lottery tickets, which is about average for many states. If they were all losers, you'd be out $200. But let's say one of the tickets came in with five out of six numbers, giving you a jackpot of $1,000. You can then deduct the $200 from your win, leaving a taxable balance of $800. Keep in mind, though, that by the time you read this book, tax laws may have changed drastically. So while I'd advise you to keep all your old lottery tickets, I also advise that you consult a tax expert to see whether you can use them for deductions.

HINT 12: Take the time to study the various odds and prize structures of your state's games.

It's impossible for me to go into all the various odds and prizes of each state. It would take the entire book, and probably change by the time you read this. So you have to do some homework on your own. In reviewing the games, ask yourself a few important questions:

- Which games have the best overall odds of winning?
- What's the best ratio between the odds and the prize? (In other words, what games give the best bang for the buck?)
- Does the lottery in a nearby state have much better odds? Should I be playing there instead of where I live?
- Are there any special rules or regulations that I should be aware of?
- How long do I have before I need to claim my prize?

HINT 13: Collect your winnings as soon as possible.

How'd you like to be one of those lucky few people who have won the lottery, only to wait too long to claim your prize? It's happened a number of times, and lottery officials are adamant: If the rules of your state say you have 180 days to claim your prize, and you show up on day 181, you're out of luck. That's exactly what happened to a couple who, because of their immigration status, waited until the day after the deadline to try to collect a $200,000 win. They didn't collect a penny.

Believe it or not, there have been many cases where people knowingly waited before collecting their prize money. In the case of huge jackpots, it does make sense to consult with an attorney and a good accountant before cashing in. That's fine. But some people have actually waited so long that they lose their prizes. In one case, a gentleman who had won almost $140,000 waited so long that he forgot where he'd put the winning ticket. By the time he finally found it—in the glove compartment of his car—the deadline had passed. So the lesson from this is to not dawdle. Cash in that ticket as soon as you feel comfortable coming forward.

HINT 14: If you do play the same numbers on a regular basis, make sure not to miss a week.

Although this bit of advice might not increase the odds of winning, it may save you a great deal of grief. You may have heard the story that follows: "A friend of a friend of mine played the same numbers every week for seven years. But one weekend, she had to go to a funeral and, wouldn't you know it, her numbers finally came up, but she hadn't bought a ticket!" I have yet to confirm such a story, but it is good advice, nonetheless, to play your numbers until, for whatever reason, you decide to stop. As I mentioned, I've been playing my numbers for years and never miss a game.

CHAPTER 4

Sweepstakes: You Really Can Be a Winner!

MAKE NO MISTAKE ABOUT IT, sweepstakes are games of luck. But you'd be amazed by how much you can improve your chances of winning them. By reading this book carefully, you'll be able to avoid most of the silly mistakes that immediately disqualify up to 50 percent of your competitors. Imagine how much less you'll need to rely on luck if you don't make any of those mistakes.

Anybody can win a sweepstakes. No special skills are required. Unlike a contest, you don't have to have a way with words, a knack for cooking, or any particular ability. This is why the people who've won sweepstakes have come from such diverse backgrounds. Rich people, poor people, college graduates, high school dropouts, men, women, young people, and old people have all been winners. Therefore, theoretically speaking, everyone has exactly the same chance of winning.

But do they really? Not exactly. Before your heart sinks, let me reassure you that it's a good thing that not everyone has an equal chance. You see, the odds are not made unequal due to any kind of natural bias inherent to sweepstakes; the odds are made unequal by people who know how to play smart (which is true of just about anything in life, when you think about it). And by the time you put this book down, you'll know how to play smart. Luckily for us, a great change is taking place with regard to sweepstakes: the prizes are getting bigger. These days, it is not uncommon for a house or an expensive sports car to be given away. Cash prizes are also growing in size, and there are now, more than ever, sweepstakes out there that offer a million dollars or more in cash.

Also growing in popularity are the number of sweepstakes that require the winner to perform a certain task in order to win. These types of sweepstakes often focus on a certain sporting act, such as sinking a putt, kicking a field goal, or making a basket from half court. And because the task could net a hefty prize for the contestant, it is in the best interest of the winners to train for weeks for their big day. If you're going to enter these kinds of sweepstakes, you should at least have some skill at the designated task. And if you have a friend or family member who you think could perform the feat, enter him or her instead.

Normally, however, after you enter a sweepstakes, your work is pretty much done. But the company's work has just begun. The winners of most sweepstakes are picked through random drawings. There are usually several drawings, as too many people enter for all the entry forms to fit into one bag or drum. Several entry forms are usually picked by a blindfolded person from each mail sack that the company receives and then these forms are put into a barrel. Another blindfolded person picks the winners from these forms. Some sweepstakes now assign each entrant a number, which is entered into a computer upon receipt of the entry form. The computer then randomly selects the winning numbers.

Almost all companies use independent judging organizations to be responsible for picking the winners. This makes some people very nervous; they think that the judges can get away with giving the prizes to friends and relatives. But, rest assured, this never happens. Such organizations are highly reputable firms, and if they were caught cheating in a sweepstakes, they would not only lose their business but their reputations as well. It's just not worth it.

Surprisingly, some of the prizes in sweepstakes go unclaimed by their winners. But when a prize goes unclaimed, it doesn't mean that the company hoards the prizes for themselves. It would be illegal to do so. Instead, the companies are required to hold new drawings until all the prizes have been given away. This dramatically increases your chances of being a winner.

You can always write to the company that holds the sweepstakes for a list of the winners. They'll often ask you to enclose a self-addressed stamped envelope. If participating in sweepstakes becomes your hobby, you can send away for such lists. It can take several months to receive the list, however, due to the volume of correspondence a company usually receives after holding a sweepstakes or contest.

Types of Sweepstakes

There are essentially two types of sweepstakes. The first is the direct-mail sweepstakes. A company, hoping to advertise its products to you in new and exciting ways, will send you an entry form in the mail. The companies that run this kind of promotion have usually done a lot of research on the type of people who buy their products, so they're very particular when sending out entry forms. The best known of these types of sweepstakes are the Publisher's Clearinghouse Sweepstakes and the Reader's Digest Sweepstakes. Although you may get order forms regularly, many people do not. This is an unfortunate fact of life when dealing with direct-mail sweepstakes, and unless your income or buying habits change dramatically, you'll probably have to resign yourself to the fact that you will not receive such invitations. This does not mean, of course, that you cannot enter their sweepstakes; all sweepstakes are open to everyone. However, finding out about such sweepstakes may be difficult.

The second type of sweepstakes is one that is advertised in the newspaper, a magazine, or on the container of a product you may have bought (for example, on the back of a cereal box). This kind of sweepstakes will usually ask you to send in your name and address on a card. You'll sometimes be asked to send in a proof of purchase or even just the name of the product written down on the card as well. You can usually enter this type of sweepstakes as often as you like, but be sure to read the rules. Some companies specify that you can't send more than one entry in the same envelope or package. By the way, some local sweepstakes will have an entry box where you can deposit the form, which can save you quite a bit on postage and envelopes.

In addition to these two main types of "random draw" sweepstakes, there are other formats that involve the collection of game pieces, either contained in the product itself or given away at fast food restaurants. You've probably heard of such giveaways, and may have even been given game pieces that you may have tossed. It's common for the rare winning pieces to be discarded by customers who aren't playing the game. Such sweepstakes often have unclaimed prizes and, because of this, often hold "second-chance" drawings. Keep an eye out for them, and make sure to check on applicable rules.

While we're on the subject of rules, I'd like to remind you to read them very carefully. I'll come back to this point shortly. The rules for a direct-mail sweepstakes are always enclosed with the entry form. The rules for the second type of sweepstakes will always be printed somewhere in the newspaper ad, on the product box, or entry form.

Rules and Regulations

Every promotion that you'll ever enter will have its own specific set of rules. Don't ever think that you know enough about sweepstakes to stop reading the rules! If you do, you're sure to make a host of silly, unnecessary mistakes. If there's one section of this book that you should try to commit to memory, this is the one.

Rules, like all fine print, can sometimes be difficult to understand. Obviously, it's impossible for me to explain every single set of rules in giveaways. Instead, I've analyzed the rules of several sweepstakes and compiled all the information into a set of generic guidelines. Most rules you'll encounter for sweepstakes will be very similar, so after reading over this section a couple of times, you should be able to understand any set of rules and regulations with very little difficulty.

In order to make this example as realistic as possible, I've created the name of a corporation that does not exist (at least I hope not) as the company running the sweepstakes. I've also made up the date of the deadline for entry. So don't enter!

RULE 1: Greetings from the Yummy-Yum Candy Corporation. To enter our fabulous new sweepstakes, you may either use our official entry form or you can use a 3 x 5 inch plain piece of paper.

Most sweepstakes print official entry forms, but they often say you can substitute the form with a piece of paper of a specific size. This size is usually 3 x 5 inches. Promotions are usually very specific about what you can use as a substitute for the entry form; some say a piece of paper, some say an index card. Always be sure to use the correct substitute. Furthermore, some promotions, such as the example given above, say the piece of paper (or card, in other promotions) must be plain. That means no lines.

It's probably a good idea for you to go to the store and buy cards and papers in a variety of sizes, some lined and some unlined, so that you're prepared to enter any sweepstakes that come your way. I shop at office supply stores and buy in bulk, both to cut down on expense and on trips to the store.

Never send a post card in as a entry unless the rules specifically state that this is an acceptable substitute for the entry form. Moreover, never photocopy the entry form unless the rules indicate that you may do so. Each year judges throw out hundreds of entries that could have been winners because the entrant assumed it would be okay to use a photocopy of the entry form.

RULE 2: Hand print your name and address on the entry form or on the piece of paper. Print in block letters.

This means that you shouldn't type up the entry form. Only type it if the rules specifically say that you can do so. It also means that you're not allowed to hand write it in cursive. The rule for this is obvious: if your handwriting is sloppy, the judges won't be able to read it. This rule says to hand print your information in block letters, so that's what you should do. Block letters are large capital letters that are easy to read. Here's an example of what I mean:

THESE ARE BLOCK LETTERS

Always print your full name. Do not use any aliases or nicknames, as winners are usually required to furnish proof of identification. Always print your full address, including your apartment number and zip code. Small mistakes such as these could cost you thousands of dollars.

RULE 3: Send your entry in a hand-printed envelope.

Again, hand print the company's address as well as your return address. Do not type or write in cursive unless they indicate that you may do so—labeled or rubber-stamped return addresses are often permitted. It is vital that you write as neatly as possible. When I first started entering sweepstakes, I made the mistake of scribbling out as many envelopes as I could. The results were sloppy and also took away from the enjoyment of the process.

Also be sure to print the sweepstakes company's address exactly as it appears in the rules. If you find several sweepstakes company addresses in the rules, then use any of them. Sometimes companies give several addresses and monitor the quantity of mail they receive at each address. This has no effect on the outcome of the sweepstakes, but it does allow the company to determine if certain typefaces in their advertisements attract a reader's attention better than others.

You may use any size envelopes unless rules indicate otherwise. Most experienced entrants use a long, white #10 business envelope, but you can use a smaller envelope if you prefer. I'll use a larger envelope if I feel a blindfolded judge has a better chance of grabbing onto it. The problem, however, is that larger envelopes are also more expensive.

RULE 4: Enclose the wrapper from a Yummy-Yum Deluxe Bon-Bon with your entry, or hand print in block letters the words "Yummy-Yum Deluxe Bon-Bon" on a separate 3 x 5 inch plain piece of paper.

Since this is a sweepstakes, the company is not allowed to demand that you buy their product as a condition of entering the promotion. Therefore, you really don't have to enclose a wrapper. If you choose to print the words, again remember that you're not allowed to type or write in cursive unless the rules specifically allow you to do so. The quotation marks surrounding the words may or may not be necessary, but put them in just in case (unless the rules say that you shouldn't). Note that this promotion's rules indicate to print the words on a separate piece of paper. Some will ask you to print them on the same piece of paper with your name and address. Be sure to follow this rule carefully. Moreover, if the rules indicate to print the words on a separate piece of paper, do not attach it to the piece of paper with your name and address unless the rules tell you to do so. If they want the two pieces of paper attached, then they will usually be very specific about how you should attach them.

RULE 5: Enter as often as you wish, but mail all entries separately. All entries must be received by February 8, 2025.

If the rules allow you to enter as many times as you want, then by all means do so. If you plan to enter many times, then you will soon realize how handy it is to have a supply of various index cards and pieces of paper on hand. Don't worry about entering too often. Even if a judge sees your name a million times, he or she is not allowed to throw away any eligible entry. There's no such thing as promotion "blacklisting." That would be illegal.

You must mail your entries separately. There's no use in sending ten thousand entries if you pack them in the same envelope or box, because they'll all be disqualified. This means that you may have to spend quite a bit of money on postage, but you simply can't get away with breaking the rules.

This rule also indicates that entries must be received by February 8, 2025. If a rule is phrased in a similar manner, then it is a good idea to mail your entry at least 1 week to 10 days before the date given. This gives you some time if there's any delay in the mail. Some rules say that entries must be postmarked by a certain date; that means that you can wait until that very day to put your entry in the mailbox, as the post office will postmark your envelope later that day.

RULE 6: Winners are determined by a random drawing.

This means exactly what it says. Certain sweepstakes may indicate that winners are determined randomly by computer.

RULE 7: No substitutions will be made in awarding prizes. Only one prize per household. All prizes will be awarded.

Sweepstakes almost never let you choose the prize you win. So it's just common sense to enter only those sweepstakes that offer things you might like to have. Remember, a sweepstakes isn't worth entering if you wouldn't buy the prizes for either yourself or someone else as a gift. Unwanted prizes can sometimes be surprisingly difficult to get rid of. Many "unlucky" winners have received prizes they did not want, and were unable to sell, but they still had to pay taxes on them. Imagine losing money by winning a promotion! For example, a cable television station was offering a trip around the world, including stops in New York, London, Bangkok, and San Francisco—all in just eight days. The total value? A whopping 35,000 taxable dollars. Can you even afford to pay what might be more than $12,000 in taxes?

Sometimes incomplete prizes are even offered. For example, they may offer a vacation but not pay the airfare. Is this really the kind of prize you want? If it's something you don't really want for yourself, you might enter anyway in hopes of winning the prize for a friend or relative. If it turns out to be a prize they don't want either, then you still have the option of forfeiting the prize.

Usually, only one prize is awarded per household. This means that if three unrelated people who all live at exactly the same address all win prizes in the same sweepstakes, only one will be allowed to collect his or her prize. If this ever happens, the company may disqualify all three entrants. If a single individual wins more than one prize, then the company has the right to choose which prize the person gets to keep. Some rules specify that only one prize is allowed per family, rather than per household.

The rules usually indicate that all prizes will be awarded. As I mentioned earlier, this means that the judges will continue to hold drawings until all the prizes have been given away.

RULE 8: Winning odds are determined by the number of entries received.

The more eligible entries the sweepstakes receives, the smaller your chance of winning. If a million people enter, the odds are a million to one. If five hundred thousand entries are received, the odds are five hundred thousand to one. You get the picture.

RULE 9: Winners must take all responsibility for local, state, and federal taxes on their prizes.

Occasionally (but very rarely) a sweepstakes will pay the taxes for the winners. It's a nice, albeit rare, occurrence. Taxation of winnings will be discussed in more detail in a later chapter, but it's important to note it here as well. Remember that ugly piece of furniture you won? You still have to pay taxes on it, even if you can't sell it to anyone, so you could actually end up losing money.

RULE 10: Sweepstakes are open to the residents of the continental United States. Entrants must be at least 18 years of age. Employees and families of the employees of the Yummy-Yum Candy Corporation, the independent judging firm, and the advertising agency are not eligible. Void where prohibited.

These are the final eligibility requirements for winning a prize. Even if you've done everything else correctly, if you don't meet these requirements, you will not receive a prize. Companies that sponsor sweepstakes are very careful to make sure that these requirements are met, so don't even bother trying to lie.

Note that this rule indicates that the sweepstakes is only open to residents of the continental U.S. If you live in Alaska, you're out of luck. If you live in Hawaii, you're out of luck. If you live in Puerto Rico, you're out of luck. The geographic requirements of different sweepstakes sometimes vary greatly, so be sure to read this rule carefully. This sweepstakes requires you to be at least 18 years old. Some say that you must be at least 16, and some say at least 21. Again, double check to make sure you qualify.

If you or anyone in your family works for any of the companies listed in the rules, then you're also out of luck. These exclusion rules vary according to sponsors but they usually include parents, children, spouses, siblings, and persons living in the same household. Sometimes, even spouses of siblings or siblings of spouses are excluded. Sorry, but that's the way it is.

And by now we all know what "void where prohibited" means.

That's a pretty complete set of rules. They are not strict, nor are they especially complicated, but they are complete. If you can understand them, then you should be able to understand the rules of any promotion. And if you can understand the rules, then you can be sure not to make the simple mistakes that eliminate as many as 50 percent of the entrants! Don't you feel like your chances of winning are better already?

CHAPTER 5

Contests: Games of Skill

CONTESTS ABSOLUTELY REQUIRE more skill than sweepstakes. There are several types of contests, but most require the contestant to write a rhyme or a slogan. Many, but not all, contests require a proof of purchase from a product.

Companies are sometimes reluctant to sponsor contests, usually opting in favor of sweepstakes, for several reasons. In the past, companies have run into legal problems and have had to state in court why they felt one slogan was better than another. While this is a very rare occurrence—and to my knowledge neither a company nor its judging organization has ever lost such a court battle—contests always result in many disgruntled people who honestly feel that they provided the best entry. In fact, companies are inevitably swamped by letters from these people, demanding an explanation for their loss; as you can imagine, this is not the kind of positive advertising that a company hopes to generate by holding a promotion. Moreover, contests usually fail to attract a large number of entrants, as many people feel they do not possess the talent needed to win.

But contests are becoming more common. The reasons for this are simple. First, whereas sweepstakes have been opposed at various times by local and federal legislators, people rarely have any suspicions about a contest due to the fact that skill is required. And, secondly, a really good entry in a contest could result in a very successful ad campaign for a company; rather than pay experts to come up with a catchy slogan, why not ask you to do it for free?

People often get upset when they discover that they have to purchase a product in order to enter, but this is quite silly. How could you ever write a jingle or slogan if you have never even used the product? The judges can usually tell which contestants are truly familiar with the product, and they immediately disqualify those that are not; in fact, contests often stipulate that sincerity is one of the qualities that the judges look for when selecting the best entry. If this seems unfair to you in any way, it shouldn't. After all, companies are looking for a contestant who can paint the smallest details of a product in the most appealing light. For example, a company that makes dish-washing detergent might want you to describe how effortlessly their product works and how wonderful it smells, not just that it cleans dishes.

As with sweepstakes, a list of the contest's winners is available upon demand, usually several months after the contest is over. But don't ask the company to send you a copy of the winning slogan because they will usually refuse to do so. You might want to see the winning entry so that you can get a better idea of what contest sponsors look for in a slogan or jingle, but you must remember that the judges have to make subjective decisions. Contest writing is a creative process, not a science, and as a result, some entries will simply appeal to the judges more than others. Companies realize this, and they do not want to alienate you by revealing a winning entry that you feel is inferior to your own.

It is worthwhile to point out that being a serious contestant requires a tremendous amount of devotion on your part. Don't just think you can whip out a catchy phrase after a few hours. Were it that simple, then advertising agencies wouldn't have multimillion dollar contracts with corporations. You've got to practice your skills at every possible moment, occupying your spare time by trying to invent new jingles for the products you use. But don't be scared by the amount of effort you must exert. I cannot tell you how fulfilling it is to write a catchy phrase or create a new tune. As with all things in life, the contests that take the most time are also the most rewarding.

Also, an advantage to entering written contests is that most people don't bother because they believe that too much effort is necessary to come up with a winning entry. This lessens your competition! There is no need to be a literary scholar, master chef or expert in any field to become a contest winner; often novices approach contests with a fresh perspective. Of course, it helps to have the edge of knowing the tips in my book!

Types of Contests

There are two major types of contests. First, there are word contests, which ask you to create a rhyme, slogan, jingle, caption, or to explain why you use a certain product in a limited number of words. Second, there are recipe and cooking contests, in which you're asked to create simple yet delicious culinary delights.

The best thing about the word contests is that the sponsor usually indicates what criteria the judges use to rate an entry. Again, as contests help the sponsor with advertising, they are looking for strong writing skills. They don't want to trick you or prevent you from creating a masterpiece. So if a word contest's rules say that you should stress "clarity, originality, and sincerity," then you should be clear, original, and sincere.

The key to being a successful word contester is to follow the old "S.O.S." rule. This rule means you should be "Simple, Original, and Sincere." And, as always, remember to follow the rules!

Recipe promotions are the second major type of contest. They have one distinct advantage over word contests: You don't need to learn a new skill in order to participate. Whereas most of you are probably not writers, almost all of you have spent time in the kitchen. You all have secret family recipes handed down to you from your parents and grandparents. Chances are good that there's at least one dish you prepare every so often, perhaps when you have guests over, that everyone loves. It's possible that this very dish could win you thousands of dollars.

I want to stress at this point that recipe contests are not the sole domain of women. More and more men are beginning to enter the kitchen, and many are discovering a remarkable talent for concocting delicious meals. Historically, many of the big winners of cooking contests have been women, but recently, men have had some startling victories. So, if you are a man, don't think that you have to skip this section of the book. As a matter of fact, Kurt Wait from Redwood City, California won the grand prize of $1 Million in the Pillsbury Bake-Off in 1996 with his Macadamia Fudge Torte recipe.

I'll discuss specific strategies to help you with cooking contests later in this chapter, but I'd like to give you a few hints now. In advertising, presentation is at least as important as content. Since contests are a form of advertising, this rule holds true for contests as well. Even if you have a delicious new recipe, you might not get very far if you don't present it well to the judges. You have to send in a recipe that looks and sounds so delicious that it will make the judges' mouths water just by reading it. You're probably thinking that you should try to make recipes that the judges will want to eat themselves, and you are right.

The problem is trying to figure out what they want to eat. It is obviously impossible to predict what flavors someone enjoys, so the best thing for you to do is research what kinds of dishes have won contests recently. In order to do this, you will probably have to subscribe to a national magazine such as *Family Circle*, which regularly publishes winning recipes. Compare the ingredients from each. Compare the methods of cooking and necessary preparation time. Look for similarities. There aren't that many independent judging organizations in this country, so it is only natural that the same people often judge many contests. Therefore, with a little research, you should be able to find some clues as to what will be well-received.

But this is not to say that you should merely copy another recipe, or simply make a slight variation of it, because this will result in your immediate disqualification. Originality is just as important in cooking as it is in word contests. With recipes, you should always follow the old "S.O." rule: "Simple and Original." You need to present a dish that is easy to make, uses inexpensive ingredients that are easy to find, and tastes delicious. And don't forget, you need to present it with flair!

Word Contests

The rules for most word contests specify that your entry will be judged for its aptness of thought, originality, sincerity, and clarity. Moreover, the rules usually indicate, in percentages, how much attention will be paid to each of these traits; sincerity, for example, is often rated over 25 percent. But what exactly does this mean, and how can you tailor your entry to stress these qualities? That's what this section is all about. Being specific is important because the company sponsoring the contest wants to find out what you specifically like about the product. Therefore, your entry must be highly specific, suggesting particular qualities of the product you are writing about. In other words, if your entry describes toothpaste just as aptly as it describes self-sealing tires, then chances are it won't win. It is also important to remember that you're trying to endorse a specific company's product. Don't just rattle on about why brushing with fluoride toothpaste is important. Instead, clearly indicate why brushing your teeth with "Bright-n-Shiny" brand toothpaste is important.

There's a very good chance that you might never have used some of the products that you hope to write about, and you can't even try to write about them without knowing their virtues. As a result, if you don't already own the product, you might have to invest some of your hard-earned money in buying one for each contest you wish to enter. I realize that this may initially seem like a terrible thing to have to do, but remember that you're required to devote a certain amount of time and money to any hobby if you wish to succeed at it. If you're going to enter a contest for "Bright-n-Shiny" fluoride toothpaste, go out and buy a tube. Brush your teeth with it. What does it taste like? Does it leave more or less grit in your mouth than your regular brand does? What color is it? How does it smell? Does it lather up a lot or a little? You must be aware of these things. And, you never know, you may even discover that you actually like this brand better.

When advertisers try to market a product, they make lists of qualities known as sales points. For example, a sales point of "Bright-n-Shiny" might be that it tastes better than another leading fluoride toothpaste. So when you sit down to enter a contest, you might want to approach it by listing the sales points. This can be quite a time-consuming process, and it raises an interesting point: You will be able to complete such a list more quickly and, therefore, enter more contests if you write about things with which you are somewhat familiar. Thus, if you know absolutely nothing about lawn care, and aren't really interested in learning anything about it, then you may want to steer clear of contests for gardening products.

I'll return to sincerity, originality, and clarity (simplicity) later in this chapter, but for now, I would like to discuss ways in which you should describe the sponsor's product.

Any successful writer needs a variety of reference books. This is true for the greatest of artists, such as Shakespeare, as well as for the contest entrant. I certainly wouldn't have been able to write this book without my own personal reference library. But what constitutes a library? Many scholars equip themselves with The Oxford English Dictionary, a tremendous volume (now sold on computer disk) that not only defines words but also places them in the context of great works of art. The Oxford English Dictionary's entry for the word "tragedy," for example, makes reference to Shakespeare's Romeo and Juliet. These scholars are also sure to have on hand a dictionary of synonyms and antonyms, so that they can expand their comprehension of various words. Many also like to have a reputable encyclopedia, a rhyming dictionary, and a book of quotations.

But do you really need all of that? Of course not. All you need is a good dictionary and a good thesaurus. You can usually buy both of them in a set for about $20 or $30, and they're well worth the expense. Don't buy the small paperback copies, as they are not very thorough. Do yourself the favor of investing in the large hard-cover copies.

You should use the dictionary as a foundation for your writing. Refer to it whenever you have questions about spelling and usage. But also refer to it throughout the process of making the list of sales points. You may be able to find several meanings for some of the words you put on the list, which will allow you to make a pun in your slogan (which judges often seem to like). The large hard-cover dictionaries sometimes include antonyms as well, enabling you to contrast your words with their opposites. The thesaurus also comes in handy when making the list, as you'll find many synonyms which will give your writing the flair it needs to win.

Once you've got the books, you'll be able to use language to its fullest advantage. But I cannot stress enough that the key to being a successful writer is to practice; no hints that I can give you will be of any use if you don't practice your writing skills. Think of anyone you have ever seen who is incredibly skillful—a basketball player, a race car driver, an archer, a poet, a physicist. One of the reasons they seem to achieve their goals so effortlessly is that they've spent countless hours practicing.

In order to communicate effectively in your entry, you've got to have something to say. But you must also say it with style. If you can do this, then you stand a good chance of winning. But how can you develop a style of your own? By following some of the suggestions below, you should be able to write with considerable pizzazz. Incidentally, this list of suggestions is by no means exhaustive, so if you can think of any that I've forgotten, then don't hesitate to add them.

Comparisons: There are two types of comparisons that you can make between things. The first is the simile. Similes compare two things by using the words "like" or "as." For example, "Her tears fell like rain" is a simile. The second type is the metaphor. Metaphors are considered slightly more sophisticated than similes because they dispense with "like" or "as" and simply imply the comparison. An example of this could be, "The race car driver was a bird of prey." The strength of metaphors is illustrated even in this example. By omitting the words "like" or "as," it adds intensity to the sentence. You can really imagine the race car driver swooping around the track, desperately trying to catch up with and overtake all of his opponents, hungering to win the grand prize. Try reading the example again but this time include the word "like." You see? It loses much of its force. For this reason, judges tend to prefer metaphors to similes.

Metaphors have an added advantage in that they can more easily convey action than similes, which is another thing that attracts judges. For example, in the previous paragraph I wrote, "You can really imagine the race car driver swooping around the track." This is also a metaphor, as it implies a connection between the driver and the bird. And a final advantage is that they are slightly shorter. When asked to describe why you love "Bright-n-Shiny" toothpaste in 25 words or less, a single word could be crucial.

Personification: Personification is a special type of metaphor in which inanimate objects are compared to living creatures, usually people. Thus, "The race car driver swooped around the track" is not personification but "The race car swooped around the track" is. This is possibly the single most important language technique that you will use in your entries. You will probably be able to use it in every single contest you enter. You can describe how a stain remover works by writing "Clean-O stain remover eats stains away." You can describe the toothpaste by writing "Bright-n-Shiny brushes plaque away." And if you look carefully at advertisements from now on, I'm sure that you will discover that professional ad campaigns rely heavily on personification. Think how many times you've seen talking bubbles or maple syrup jugs on TV commercials.

Alliteration: This is a technique in which many of the words in a sentence start with the same letter (technically, if the letter is a vowel, then it is called "assonance," and if the letter is a consonant then it is called "consonance"). Judges are also generally attracted to this. You have to be very careful with this technique, however, as it easily begins to sound dumb. If you write, "Poker brand Popsicles pack a powerful yet pleasing punch," then you are bound to annoy the judges. Subtlety is the key. Try to limit your alliteration to three or four words, and if you intersperse them throughout a sentence, then you could give your entry a pleasing ring that will delight the judges.

Typos: Typos (those done on purpose, that is) can also be amusing. If you can somehow work such a technique into your entry, then it could help you become a winner. If you are entering a contest sponsored by Luscious brand snack foods, then you might want to declare their cupcakes: "De-Luscious." But, as you can see by this example, you have to be very careful when using this; it can seem extremely corny. So only use this technique when you really feel it will improve your entry.

Rhymes: Although rhymes can be useful in any contest, they tend to work best in jingles. But, as with any other technique, they must be used sparingly. The rules of some contests specifically tell you to avoid rhymes, whereas others encourage it. Rhyming almost always goes hand in hand with meter, or rhythm. If you try to say some rhymes in your head, you'll probably notice yourself talking in a singsong voice. This is another reason why rhyming is usually best saved for jingles.

Puns: This can be a very effective technique for grabbing the judges' attention. Puns allow your entry to have a double meaning, but you must remember to keep such puns simple. Never allude to literary masterpieces that many people haven't read. Never allude to a foreign language, which is bound to confuse not only the general public but the judges as well.

There are really two types of puns. First, there are implied puns, in which the words in a sentence can be interpreted more than one way. These are the most difficult to achieve and are, therefore, often the favorite of judges. Second, there are puns in which you create a variation on a word. These are somewhat easier to make, but they can sometimes be very effective. For example, you might want to advertise a Renaissance Fair using the words "Knight Life."

Grouping: Grouping usually occurs in pairs or triads (groups of three). Although the two have a very similar effect, you construct them in entirely different ways. Pairs generally involve opposites that balance out a phrase. Many years ago a contestant won a fortune with the entry: "A winner never quits, and a quitter never wins." As impressive as pairing may seem, triads are even more so. Rather than oppose each other, however, the words in triads sometimes support each other. Take words from your list of sales points and try to combine them in interesting ways. One famous triad was used as the name of a Clint Eastwood movie in the early '70s: *The Good, The Bad, and the Ugly*. Note that these words seem to work with each other; you'll probably find this technique most effective when combining it with another, such as alliteration. This technique is probably the most difficult one to achieve, so if you have some success with it you should feel very proud of yourself.

The Heart-Warming Story: You might also want to share something touching about your own life, not so much to gain the judge's sympathy, but to strengthen the product's appeal. It's yet another way of getting a positive response from the judges, who may look at hundreds of entries per day. Let's say you're writing a jingle for a dog food company. Why not mention that your Labrador just had eight puppies and LabChow dog food has kept her healthy and happy? Such a story is not only heart warming but also helps sell the product. What you don't want to do is go overboard and say that all the puppies had worms. Heart warming is good; tear jerking is bad.

Now that you understand the ways in which you can create a style, let's return to the basic rules of simplicity, originality, and sincerity. As I've said, you must use these techniques as sparingly and simply as possible, or else they will lose their punch and become tiresome. I've already discussed sincerity, or the ability to convincingly praise a certain brand of product through your experience with it. So now we're left with originality.

Judges consider originality to be the ability to express your ideas in a unique way. All of the techniques you have just read about will certainly help you to be original, but you also need to approach each contest from a new angle. If you're asked to write a slogan for "Bright-n-Shiny" toothpaste, rather than discuss its cavity-fighting ability, perhaps you could think about the fresh breath it creates. From there, you can conclude what kind of an effect this will have on a person's romantic life and come up with the slogan, "Lovers love Bright-n-Shiny toothpaste." Hopefully your entries will be better than that, but you get the idea.

Recipe Contests

Not surprisingly, the judges of recipe contests also consider originality to be a major factor in their decision. In fact, most entries are eliminated immediately because they aren't original; sometimes they are straight rip-offs of old recipes, and other times they are so close to old recipes that they might as well be rip-offs. Remember, your recipe must be significantly different from any other in order to be a contender. A minor change in the ingredients or their amounts is not different enough. But, surprisingly, you can make a recipe that tastes very similar to an old favorite if you have a new, easy way to prepare it. Here's an example of a Pillsbury Bake-Off winner by Linda Rahman, which, as we'll see, is a classic example of what judges are looking for:

Blueberry-Poppy Seed Brunch Crunch
Preparation Time: 15 minutes
Baking Time: 45 to 55 minutes

⅔ cup granulated sugar
½ cup butter or margarine, softened
2 teaspoons grated lemon peel
1 large egg
1 ½ cups all-purpose Pillsbury flour
2 tablespoons poppy seeds
½ teaspoon baking soda
¼ teaspoon salt
½ cup sour cream

Filling
Two cups fresh or frozen blueberries, thawed
⅓ cup granulated sugar
2 teaspoons all-purpose flour
¼ teaspoon nutmeg

Glaze
⅓ cup confectioners' sugar
1 to 2 teaspoons milk

Preheat oven to 350 degrees Fahrenheit. Grease and flour bottom and sides of 9" or 10" spring-form pan. Beat sugar and butter in bowl until fluffy. Add lemon peel and egg, beat at medium speed for two minutes. Combine flour, poppy seeds, baking soda, and salt. Add to butter mixture alternately with sour cream, beginning and ending with flour mixture.

Spread batter over bottom and one inch up sides of pan, so the batter on all sides is ¼ inch thick.

Filling: Combine all ingredients in medium bowl. Sprinkle over batter.

Bake 45 to 55 minutes, until cake is golden brown. Cool slightly. Remove sides from pan. Drizzle top with glaze. Serve warm or cool. Makes 8 servings.

Glaze: Combine confectioners' sugar and milk in bowl. Blend until smooth.

Linda Rahman's recipe caught the judge's attention for a number of reasons. Let's break it down: Ease of preparation is an extremely important criterion in cooking contests, often being of equal or greater importance to originality. However, don't think that your dish has to have less than five ingredients in order to be considered easy. In fact, many winning dishes have many ingredients, but they're straight-forward. These recipes don't call for any elaborate methods of preparation, such as dicing fish into perfect one-inch cubes, sautéing them in butter for just under 52 seconds, and adding two drops of vanilla extract exactly 12 ½ seconds into the procedure. It's even recommended that you substitute "ready-to-serve" ingredients whenever possible; if your recipe calls for chicken stock, then use stock from a can, rather than making some from scratch. A good guideline for determining ease of preparation is to ask yourself whether or not you would be willing to make it after coming home from a long day at work. As you can see, Rahman's recipe is not as simple as a box of macaroni and cheese, but it is most certainly accessible to the average cook.

All recipe contests will stipulate that you use a certain ingredient in your dish. After all, this is a form of advertising for their product. Therefore, if you're entering a contest sponsored by Yummy Yum Chocolates, then they'll ask you to use at least one of their candy bars in the recipe. Never use less than the amount they ask you to use. If possible, use even more, as this will impress the judges. In general, winning entries use more than the minimum amount. Clearly, Rahman lived up to this requirement by making flour the main ingredient of her recipe.

Another important factor is cost. Are the ingredients expensive? Contest sponsors usually look for recipes that will appeal to people on a tight budget, so don't bother sending in a delightful way to prepare lobster tail. And don't think that the judges will be interested in trying something new and expensive; they always want to taste something original and different, but they're usually given strict limits by the contest sponsor as to how expensive the dish can be.

There is only one exception to this rule but, in general, I would not even recommend this. If your recipe does call for an expensive ingredient, and if there is no cheaper substitute for that ingredient, then you can submit the recipe so long as the leftovers can be saved. If your ingredients must be consumed immediately, then don't bother. Again, Rahman's recipe consists of simple, inexpensive ingredients.

A third factor is the availability of the ingredients. If your recipe calls for an obscure spice that is only cultivated every ninth month in southern China, then don't bother submitting it, no matter how good it tastes. In this sense, availability of the ingredients is related very closely with cost. A good way of insuring availability of ingredients is to use ingredients that are available at any national supermarket chain. This will eliminate the possibility of any items being available only in certain regions of the country. Traditionally, winning recipes have been those in which normal ingredients result in a fabulous taste, and this is one way in which you should never break with tradition. Again, if you buy canned and other already prepared foods, you'll help guarantee availability.

Remember to experiment with new flavor combinations. Improve upon a favorite recipe, making it more healthful. Create a new look for a familiar food. Play with the very idea of the dish: Create an appetizer out of a main dish or a dessert out of a snack. Substitute convenience ingredients for several ingredients in an old recipe.

And you can't be shy about having people around you test the recipe. I've found that family and friends can often provide unbiased feedback when it comes to food, as long as you realize that everyone has different preferences and that you can't please them all. You can ask the following questions, and if you see a pattern forming, take note. In general, does it taste good? Is it too bland or spicy? Is the texture pleasing? You should also try to look at the recipe in terms of universal appeal. Will it appeal to the whole family? Would it appeal to Americans in general? Is it a recipe that people would make often?

There are some recipe contests that call for ethnic foods, but you should try to ensure the availability of ingredients as much as possible even for these promotions. Just because you're making an Italian dish doesn't mean you should have to travel to Italy to find the things you need. Explore your own ethnic heritage in the comfort of your own kitchen. Think back to foods from your childhood and adapt them for today.

Once you've developed a delicious recipe, however, your work is far from over. In the first place, you have to think about the way to present it. Never forget the garnishing, unless the rules of the contest forbid it (always read the rules!), and always make the dish colorful and rich in texture. The recipe should look delicious, not just taste good. But never allow the look to become more important than the taste.

The final step, actually writing up the recipe, is just as important as the taste of the recipe itself. Here are a few suggestions:

SUGGESTION 1: Give clear instructions.

Don't try to be creative in the way you present your recipe. Just present it in plain language, as Rahman did for the Pillsbury Bake-Off. Save the poetry for limericks. The judges want a clear list of steps to follow in order to make your dish, not a prose paragraph detailing the history of cooking. Imagine if you were trying to assemble a piece of furniture and the instructions were difficult to read. You'd go crazy. That's pretty much how the judges feel when they don't receive a step-by-step list. If your recipe is not easy to follow, then you might as well consider yourself disqualified.

There is a standard format in which you should present your recipe. You should write the name of the recipe on the top line of the page, centered. Then skip three lines. Then list the ingredients in the order they should be used, not in order of relative importance. Then skip a few more lines and explain how to prepare the dish in straightforward, step-by-step sentences.

After completing the recipe, you should give it to one of your friends and see if they can make the dish. If they come back with any questions, or if they come back with something that looks nothing like your dish, then you should definitely rewrite the recipe.

SUGGESTION 2: Give exact measurements.

Personally, I'm the kind of cook who throws anything in a pot without stopping to think about precise measurements. But if you plan to be a recipe contest winner, then you must get into the habit of measuring exactly. Remember, the judges need to be able to reproduce your meal after reading the recipe, and if they are unsure of the proper quantities, then they'll throw your entry into the garbage.

Remember to be as specific as possible in your measurements. If your recipe calls for one tablespoon of sugar but your interpretation of a tablespoon is a huge scoop, then convert it into level tablespoons— your tablespoon, for example, may be two or three normal tablespoons. Never use personalized amounts, such as pinches or scoops, as they are different for everyone. If you use a pinch of salt, then measure it out to see exactly how much it is.

Some other things for which you must give precise measurements are the size of your pots and the temperature at which your recipe should be cooked. If your recipe calls for an ambiguous quantity, such as two large onions, then you should cut up the onions and put them in a measuring cup. That way you can avoid any uncertain terms, such as "large"; instead of telling the judges to dice two large onions, for example, you should tell them to use two cups of diced onions. It's very easy to become overly concerned with precision, as I'm sure you will discover. But, again, if you give the recipe to a friend, and the friend can make it, then you're probably being accurate enough.

SUGGESTION 3: Follow the Rules Accurately!

While this may seem like a no-brainer, many people do not follow the rules and are disqualified. Read the rules carefully, and if the rules say that you must specify farm-raised catfish in your recipe, make extra sure you only include references to farm-raised catfish.

SUGGESTION 4: Neatness counts.

I've already mentioned that recipe contests require a certain format, so follow it. Most contests ask you to type your recipe on a plain sheet of paper, 8 ½ x 11". But, as with all promotions, you should read the rules carefully. Perhaps the contest you're entering wants the recipe on index cards or perhaps it wants entries to be hand written. But whatever the format, whatever the style, make it neat. If you have a rickety old typewriter that can't print any vowels, then ask to borrow your friend's computer. If you have ugly hand printing, then ask your sister to print it out for you. For my winning chicken recipe, I used a red felt marker on green-colored paper. It may have helped an otherwise mediocre recipe get more attention than it actually deserved.

SUGGESTION 5: Highlight the contest sponsor's product.

When listing the ingredients, always type (or print) the name of the sponsor's product in capital letters. Furthermore, if you use more than the minimum amount of the product than the recipe calls for, then it is a good idea to highlight the amount as well. This is a somewhat sneaky way to catch the judges' attention, but it usually works.

You should also do a little bit of research to see what other products the company makes. For example, if the Yummy-Yum Candy Corporation is sponsoring a recipe contest in which you must use a pint of their chocolate ice cream, then look for other products made by Yummy-Yum that you can use (such as chopped nuts, chocolate syrup, etc.). Always highlight these ingredients as well as the required ingredient. Moreover, if you do some research to determine whether or not the sponsoring company is affiliated with any other companies, then you may discover more products to highlight. If, for example, you have a wonderful new recipe for a banana split, you may discover that Yummy-Yum owns the Daylight Fruit Company; in this case, not only should you list in your ingredients two cups of chopped bananas but, instead, write two cups of chopped DAYLIGHT FRUIT bananas.

This is another reason why using prepackaged ingredients can be so helpful. You are likely to stumble upon many ingredients, such as soup stocks, which are also manufactured by the sponsoring company.

SUGGESTION 6: Be careful when naming a recipe.

You have to be very careful when giving your recipe a name. Some judges prefer recipes that have straightforward names, such as "The Yummy-Yum Banana Split," whereas others prefer something more creative, such as "Banana Ecstasy." In order to figure out which type of name is more appropriate for the contest you are entering, you should do some research. Have the winners of this contest usually had straightforward names, or have they been more creative? Such research is the only way to be certain what kind of name to use.

Even when you're creative with names, however, you should always at least suggest what kind of a dish you are entering. My winning chicken entry— "Cracklin' Double-Nut Fried Chicken"—was both creative and suggestive. I believe it's a big part of the reason why I won the contest.

How do judges decide? Most recipes are judged by taste and appearance of the dish, consumer appeal, creativity, and the appropriate use of the sponsor's products.

Radio Contests

Radio contests are among the most popular of all the types of contests. While a great deal of luck is often involved—after all, the winner is often decided simply by which phone line the DJ chooses to answer—there are a few things you can do to increase your odds of winning. Try the following:

SUGGESTION 1: Be careful when using the redial function on your phone.

Using a phone with a fast redial function is very important. But if you get into a rhythm where you are hanging up right when you hear the busy signal, you could actually get through and disconnect yourself by accident! So exercise some caution, and make sure you hear that busy signal before you hang up and redial.

SUGGESTION 2: Phone features could slow you down.

Avoid having all the bells and whistles on your phone, such as call waiting and call back features. These can slow down your phone's redial function.

SUGGESTION 3: Listen to the radio during off-peak hours.

If you listen to the radio during the middle of the day when people are at work and kids are in school, early in the morning on weekends, or late at night during the week, you will have less competition when trying to get through to a radio station.

SUGGESTION 4: Use several radios.

Listen to more than one radio at a time so that you can monitor several stations at once.

SUGGESTION 5: Be aware of ratings sweeps periods.

Radio stations tend to conduct more contests during the months when their ratings are being measured. Call your local radio station and find out what months are "sweeps months." Chances are, they'll be running several contests during that period.

SUGGESTION 6: Know your trivia!

Invest in some trivia books and study up on them so that you already know or are prepared to quickly look up the answer to questions your favorite stations might ask during a contest.

SUGGESTION 7: Start a radio call-in group with your friends or relatives.

Many people form a group to monitor the different contests offered by the various radio stations in their community. Each person in the group can be responsible for keeping track of what prizes a particular station will be giving away. By using the group method, you can cover all the bases without having to listen to several stations at all hours of the day and night!

The cellular phone has obviously had a huge effect on radio contests. Now, in addition to competing with everyone listening at home, you are competing with people in their cars. On one hand, the amount of competition has been increased incrementally. On the other, better access to radio contests is available if you have a cellular phone. While a cellular phone certainly increases your chances of winning, I would like to suggest that you pull safely over to the side of the road before attempting to call.

Contest Oddities

When I was a guest on the "Maury Povich Show" on October 9, 1996, there were three other guests who had done unusual things to win prizes. In addition to these three examples of contest oddities, there were also clips played on the show of a manure diving contest and an oyster-eating contest!

Bill won $20,000 in a Jim Beam's sweepstakes in 1995. In the first part of the contest, he won a trip to New Orleans. There he competed with other sweepstakes winners in a barrel-rolling contest. He rolled a 110-pound empty barrel 50 yards in less than 10 seconds. He had trained for two months every night in the streets of Chicago.

Marcia drove to work naked in a radio station sponsored contest to win two tickets to a Duran Duran concert and backstage passes. On her way to work in the nude she was stopped by three policemen at a barricade. She was charged with indecent exposure. She had to pay a $100 fine. She got to meet members of Duran Duran after the concert.

Lance won an ATV Polaris all-terrain vehicle by sitting in mud for 72 hours in 40-degree weather in Chicago. The contest started off with nine participants. Every 4 hours he was given a 10-minute break. He started sitting in mud at 8 a.m. on a Friday morning and finished at 8 a.m. the following Monday.

In 1998, a Los Angeles radio station began taking applications for the "Sit in It and Win" contest. Four people were to sit in a new Volkswagen Beetle for two weeks straight, with only brief bathroom breaks. Cameras were even installed in the car so that the whole world could watch the progress of the four participants live on the world wide web. At the end of the two weeks, all four people remained and the station decided to break the four-way tie using the game Rock, Paper, Scissors. The station then surprised the contest participants and a large group of spectators by giving all four participants a brand-new 1998 Volkswagen Beetle.

And for possibly the most pleasant "odd" contest, if you have some spare time, and a special someone, why not kiss them . . . for an entire day. Mark and Roberta Griswold slapped each other with a big wet one for 29 hours straight. The Griswolds and their Guinness record-setting lips were flown to Paris after winning the "Breath Savers Kiss Challenge" at the Harley Davidson Cafe in New York.

Rules and Regulations

While the rules and regulations for contests are far more diverse than those for sweepstakes, there are certain hints that I can give you in order to prevent you from making silly mistakes that result in immediate disqualification. As with sweepstakes, I will provide you with a sample set of rules for a contest, but be forewarned that any rules you may come across could be totally different. This only makes sense when you consider that there are many different types of contests, asking you to perform a variety of skills, whereas all sweepstakes work in essentially the same way. I, therefore, suggest that you read this chapter very carefully, so that you can analyze all sets of regulations in the same fashion I do.

RULE 1: Greetings from the Yummy-Yum Candy Corporation, and good luck with our fabulous new contest! To enter, you must complete the last three lines of this limerick:

"There once was a Peruvian dandy,
Who loved his Yummy-Yum candy"

You've never heard of a limerick before? Don't panic. In a moment, you will get specific instructions on how to write a limerick, which is a type of poem. Right now you should concentrate on the fact that they asked you to complete three lines. That means you must write three more lines—not two, not four! Always do exactly as the rules tell you. You wouldn't believe how many poor contestants are disqualified simply because they thought it would be more creative to write a different number of lines. Usually, a word contest will specify some type of a limit. In many cases, you're asked not to exceed 25 words.

RULE 2: Using either the official entry form or a plain piece of 8½ x 11" paper, hand print your name, address, zip code, and complete the limerick. Lines three and four must rhyme, and line five must rhyme with lines one and two.

Once again you have the choice of using the official form or your own piece of paper. Note that this piece of paper is a different size than the one indicated in the sweepstakes rule, which is why I suggested buying several different types of paper. Note that it says a "plain" piece of paper, meaning unlined. And also note that it does not state that a photocopy of the official form is acceptable, so don't photocopy it.

These rules tell you to hand print. This means that you should neither type or write in cursive. Hand print only! Although it does not specify for you to do so, it's probably best for you to use block letters. Fill in your full address, including apartment number and zip code, just as the instructions ask you to do. This is exactly the same as sweepstakes. Finally, the last part of this rule explains how to write a limerick. A limerick is a special five-line poem in which certain lines rhyme with each other. Make sure that the correct lines rhyme. If you make any variations on this rhyming scheme, you'll end up with something other than a limerick. Don't be disqualified simply because you didn't read the rules closely enough. Although a limerick is the most common type of poem you'll encounter, you may be asked to write others. The rules will almost always explain the rhyming schemes of these poems.

RULE 3: All entries must be postmarked February 8, 2025. You may enter as often as you like, but each entry must be mailed separately. Mail each entry to the address on the official entry form.

These rules indicate that the entries must be postmarked by a certain date, rather than received on that date. This simply means that you must get the entry into the mailbox by that date. Although the collection times for some mailboxes are as late as 6:30 p.m., it would probably be best to drop it into the mailbox before noon. But I strongly advise against waiting until the very last day, just in case there is some kind of delay at the post office. These rules also indicate that all entries must be mailed separately. As with sweepstakes, you must not put all of your entries into a single envelope or package! If the contest doesn't stipulate what size envelope to use, then I recommend the #10 envelope (the long business envelope).

If you wish to enter more than once, then don't simply send in the same limerick several times. This is a game of skill, not of luck. Your chances of winning will only increase if you send in more than one limerick. I have heard of many people who, not really understanding the difference between a sweepstakes and contest, simply sent in the same entry over and over. If the judges don't like it once, then they certainly won't like it many times. There are an infinite number of ways to complete the three lines, so exercise your creativity and complete it as many ways as possible.

This rule also instructs you to mail your entry to the address on the entry form. If there is more than one address, then don't worry. You may remember that I explained the reason for this in the "Rules and Regulations" chapter for sweepstakes. You should probably send at least one entry to each address.

RULE 4: Send the wrapper from a Yummy-Yum candy with each entry.

Remember that skill contests can require you to include some kind of proof of purchase. There is no way around this, so don't "accidentally" leave it out, or you will be disqualified. Sometimes the rules specify a certain portion of the wrapper, such as the words "Yummy-Yum," so be careful to enclose the correct portion.

RULE 5: All entries will be judged on the following criteria: Creativity–40%; Sincerity–30%; and Specificity–30%. The decisions of the judges are final.

Contests usually specify the exact basis of their judgments. The criteria indicated above (all of which you now understand) are a good approximation of the ones you will probably encounter. If you remember to follow the "S.O.S." rule (Simple, Original, and Sincere), then you should have no trouble fulfilling the criteria. The final sentence of this rule—that all decisions are final—means that you should never bother appealing a decision. If you've lost a contest, then simply chalk it up to experience and enter a new one. Don't waste your time becoming embittered that you didn't win with an entry you thought was great. Remember, the judging process is very subjective.

RULE 6: All entries become the property of the Yummy-Yum Candy Corporation. The contest is open to residents of the contiguous U.S.A. Void where prohibited. You must be at least 18 to enter. No employees of the Yummy-Yum Candy Corporation, the judging organization, or the families of such employees are eligible. Limit one prize per family. No substitutions of prizes permitted. All prizes will be awarded. Duplicate prizes will be awarded in the case of a tie. Taxes are the responsibility of the prize winner. Entry constitutes permission to Yummy-Yum Candy Corporation for use of winners' names and photographs without further compensation.

The first sentence of this rule means that the Yummy-Yum candy corporation will own your entry after you send it to them. Thus, if they decide to use your entry as the focus of their new ad campaign, then you are not entitled to any compensation. The most that you will get is a prize. The rest of this rule is comprised of the standard disclaimers: who may or may not enter, who must pay the taxes, how many prizes you can win, where it is legal, and where it isn't, etc. As with sweepstakes, don't try to get away with cheating on any part of this rule. If you're under the age requirement, then don't enter. If you live in a state where the contest is void, then don't enter. Don't try to cheat the contest sponsor because you will be caught, and you won't receive a prize. As with most promotions, this contest prohibits you from substituting prizes. Note that this contest also stipulates that the sponsor can use your name and likeness as often as it wishes; this means that you may have to sit down for photographers if you win, and you may even see your face on the walls of the supermarket for many months.

RULE 7: For a list of winners, send a separate self-addressed stamped envelope to the address on the official entry form.

As with sweepstakes, you can request a list of the winners. But remember that you will probably not receive a copy of their entries. It may take several months for you to receive this list. Never enclose the self-addressed stamped envelope for this list with your own entry form, as this will result in your disqualification. Note that the rule specifically states to send it separately. This is usually true for all promotions, whether the rules indicate it or not.

How to Win Sweepstakes and Contests!

CHAPTER 6

BY NOW I'M SURE YOU'VE realized that there are no sure-fire ways to win a sweepstakes. This book is designed to help you maximize your potential for winning so that you won't let any opportunity pass you by. But there are certain hints that you may find useful. Perhaps, after reading this chapter, you'll have discovered a helpful hint that I've overlooked. By all means write it down immediately, since you might forget it later. It would probably even be useful to write it in the margins of this book, so that you can keep all of your information regarding sweepstakes in one place.

HINT 1: Mail to more than one address.

Earlier in the book I mentioned that sweepstakes notices sometimes list several addresses. As you now know, this is simply a monitoring device employed by the company to determine which aspect of its advertising is most effective. You can use these addresses to your advantage by mailing entries to each of them (so long as the rules indicate you may enter more than once). This way, your entry has a chance of being picked out of several mail sacks, giving you better odds of becoming the final winner.

HINT 2: Stagger your entries over the course of the sweepstakes.

Send in your entries at different points throughout the sweepstakes so that they will be thoroughly mixed into the total entries that are received. This way your entries won't all end up in one mail sack. Similarly, if a store chain is conducting a sweepstakes, try to enter in as many stores as possible. When I won the trip to Puerto Rico, I entered at over 12 different Alpha Beta supermarkets!

HINT 3: Find ways to save time for yourself.

You will soon discover that filling out hundreds of entry forms can take up hours of your time. If the rules for any sweepstakes allow you to photocopy your entries, then by all means do so (but, be warned, very few allow this). Abbreviate anything that will not be confusing to the judges; for example, write "St." rather than "Street." But never abbreviate anything that could raise a question in the judges' minds or you'll probably be disqualified. For example, never abbreviate the name of the product and never shorten your own name. By the way, self-adhesive stamps have proven to be an enormous time-saver. It also saves wear and tear on your tongue!

HINT 4: Break down the entry process into a number of steps and then perform each step in large groups.

What I mean by this is that you should not write out your entry form, put it in the envelope, write the address on the envelope, seal the envelope, attach the stamp to it, and then, finally, move on to the next entry. Doing one step at a time like this is fine if you are just sending out one letter, but when mailing things in bulk, it becomes very time consuming. First, you should fill out all of your entry forms, index cards, or pieces of paper. Then you should address all of your envelopes and stamp them. You should then place the entries in your envelopes. Then, finally, seal them. Working in stages like this is the only way to perform such tasks without driving yourself crazy. Moreover, by dividing the process up into several jobs, you might be able to get friends or relatives to help you!

HINT 5: Put together a "sweepstakes kit" so that everything you need will be at your fingertips.

I always keep a small basket filled with everything I need to enter sweepstakes and contests. It makes the process that much simpler, faster, and more enjoyable to know that I don't have to scrounge around through my drawers looking for a stamp or a pair of scissors. Here's what I keep in my sweepstakes kit:

- Stamps for both envelopes and post cards.
- Envelopes: mostly #10, but different sizes and different colors as well.
- 3 x 5 inch cards and paper, unlined. These can be bought at any office supply store.
- Post cards of various sizes.

- Pens: Both felt tip and ball point, in several different colors.
- Stickers: While some sweepstakes may frown on this, I make it a point to have several cheery stickers (Mickey Mouse, for example) in my kit. Such stickers can get a judge's attention. However, be aware that there is a slight possibility they could gum up the high-speed mail sorters at the post office, resulting in a shredded entry.
- Upcoming sweepstakes and contest information.

HINT 6: Only enter the promotions that you are really interested in winning.

If you do your research thoroughly, you will find that there are far too many sweepstakes for you to enter them all, so only enter the ones offering prizes you really like. As I said earlier, a certain amount of selectivity will come with experience. And while many of the promotions that you enter will be the larger, national ones, don't forget about the smaller, local promotions!

HINT 7: Don't devote all of your energy to winning just one sweepstakes.

I've known of people who spend weeks and weeks filling out entry forms for a single sweepstakes. Sure, there's a logic to swamping the judges with entry forms. But I've found that it's way too discouraging to lose after spending all your time on only one promotion. I've found it's more fun (and potentially more productive) to enter a number of sweepstakes, even if you can't send in as many forms. It's less obsessive and more enjoyable.

HINT 8: Remember to check if the promotion is legal in your state, that you are old enough to enter, and you meet all other eligibility requirements.

If you don't, then don't even waste your time entering. If the promotion is illegal in your state, then don't get upset about it; it's just an annoying fact of life. You might at least want to write to your state legislators about this. If they receive enough letters, then they could seriously consider revising the laws regarding gaming in their state.

HINT 9: If rules restrict you to only one entry per person, enter for friends and relatives.

Obviously, if you're planning to enter for a friend, make sure to tell them about it, lest they get a confusing call from the promotions company announcing that they've won a trip to China. A friend of mine, for example, was confused when a radio station called and told him he'd won an expensive guitar. "Wait a second," he thought to himself, "this must have something to do with Steve." He was right. You should make arrangements in advance as to how the potential prize will be shared. Such an arrangement can help increase your odds of winning, but make sure everyone knows what's going on.

HINT 10: Try to catch the judge's eye.

This next bit of advice is somewhat controversial, but after hearing arguments—both pro and con on the subject—I now believe that sweepstakes entries should be eye-catching. Some sweepstakers go to extremes, with bright pink envelopes and dried flowers. If, as is often the case, the judge is wearing a blindfold, such extra effort is wasted. It's also wasted in contests where skill is required. But a judge is just like the rest of us. If a sweepstakes entry is attractive and bright, they might gravitate toward it. As I mentioned, I often use colored envelopes and cheery stickers to help get attention. I'll also sometimes write notes on the back of the envelopes, like "Happy Go Lucky!" Remember, though, that you should never break the rules in order to make your entry more alluring. If the rules say, "plain manila envelope" and you send in one with daisies all over it, it'll get tossed in a New York minute. Never break the rules!

HINT 11: Make the envelope or entry form "feel" different than the others.

As I mentioned a moment ago, many of the judges you'll encounter are wearing blindfolds to insure that they don't pick out an entry form from their cousin in Des Moines. So instead of submitting a colorful entry form, how about changing the "feel" of it to get noticed by the judge's fingers, if not his eyes? There are two main methods that have been used over the years by sweepstakers. The best known of these was devised by an advertising executive named Thomas Knight. Knight urged sweepstakers to fold the envelope or entry form down the middle, so that when sitting on a table it looks something like a pup tent.

The logic, of course, is that when the blindfolded judge is scrounging around for an envelope or entry form to grab, yours—which now has more shape and dimension—has a better chance of being picked.

The other popular method is known as the "accordion fold." Instead of folding the envelope or entry form one time along the middle horizontal, fold it back and forth from the edges so that it ends up looking like an accordion.

Like the horizontal fold, the ridges formed by this fold might "catch" the fingers of the judge as they rummage through a huge bag of entries. Be aware that these folding methods work better with entry forms that are simply dropped into boxes as opposed to envelopes that have to make their way through the high-speed mail sorters at the post office.

HINT 12: Enter the least-known sweepstakes and contests. The more obscure, the better. Also, play in sweepstakes that have great second or third prizes, rather than huge grand prizes.

No doubt you've already heard of Publisher's Clearing House and the Pillsbury Bake-Off. That means that millions of other people have heard of them as well; this, in turn, means that the odds against you will be greatly increased. If, on the other hand, you discover a brand-new, out-of-the-way sweepstakes that no one knows about, your entries will probably have a lot less company in the mail sack. You should also look for sweepstakes that are underadvertised, have obscure or confusing rules, and are restricted by region. I've found that the best odds are with local and regional sweepstakes with fewer entrants.

Remember, too, to enter contests not just for their big prizes but for the interesting second prizes that you have a better chance of winning. Sweepstakes that don't have behemoth first prizes usually draw fewer entrants, which is all the better for you and me. I'm constantly on the lookout for just such sweepstakes and contests.

HINT 13: Keep track of your entries and expenses.

This isn't as hard as you might think and can be accomplished with a simple hand-written or typed piece of paper. I start by making four columns: the first column is for the name of the sweepstakes or contest; the second is the entry deadline; the third is for the draw date; and the fourth keeps track of how many entries you have mailed in. But the most difficult part of this method of organization isn't making the organizer, it's being diligent about writing down the information. This organization serves two purposes: it allows you at-a-glance updates on what you have entered and tells you when the drawing date is. This is especially important if you are staggering your entries. You can easily see when to mail that last batch of entries. The other purpose this method of organization serves is that it allows you protection against scam sweepstakes and contests. Should you receive notice about a "win," you will be able to double check the claim against those legitimate contests that you know you have entered. Another organization method that allows you to keep track of your expenses is very similar to the four-column organizer but only contains three columns: The first column is the date of the expense; the second is for the amount of the expense; and the third is for a description of the expense. Again, this organizer is only effective if you are diligent about keeping it up-to-date.

HINT 14: Visualize yourself winning the prize.

Yes, you read that correctly. I make it a point to spend a few minutes every day conjuring up an image of the prize in my mind's eye. Although this may sound strange, it has several down-to-earth benefits. First, it helps me focus on the tasks I need to perform to win the prize. Second, it makes the process all that much more enjoyable. And the more I enjoy it, the more forms I'll fill out. The more forms I fill out, the better my chances of winning! Besides the practical side of it, I do believe that visualizing the prize sends out a lot of positive energy, which never hurts. I must be doing something right, since I keep on winning!

HINT 15: Enter Sweepstakes and contests that have short deadlines.

The less time people have to enter, the fewer the people who enter. The fewer the people who enter, the better your odds. It's also advisable to enter during the summer months and over holidays, since potential entrants will be occupied with kids at home, vacations, and relatives. Another great time to enter is right after postage rates go up, since many people are reluctant to use the more expensive postage at first.

HINT 16: Have fun!

This is the single most important hint I can give you. Entering sweepstakes and contests should be enjoyable, not some kind of desperate act that you're forced into because you need money. If you find that the tasks involved in winning are just no fun, or that you're spending more on postage than you should, then you might want to consider a new hobby. With that said, however, I'd advise you to stick with it for at least six months. That's how long it may take to become a winner, and then you'll be hooked!

CHAPTER 7

Where to Look for Lotteries, Sweepstakes, and Contests

THERE'S AN OLD SAYING that goes, "Luck is where preparation meets opportunity." So when will opportunity knock? When will you get the chance to turn your sweepstakes preparation into luck?

Never!

Let me repeat myself: never! Opportunity won't knock on your door. You have to go out and hunt down opportunity where it lives, without anyone's help. In other words, you've got to make your own breaks. It's a piece of wisdom that's often overlooked or forgotten, but we pay a steep price when we don't abide by its rule. This is true of just about everything else in life, so why shouldn't it be true of sweepstakes?

So where do you go in order to find opportunity? Where can you go to find all the sweepstakes? Believe it or not, the fact that you probably don't know the answer is very good news indeed. Because if you don't know, then that probably means most other people don't know either. Fact is, companies across the country hold thousands of sweepstakes every year, but most people miss out on them because they just don't know where to look. But if you read through some of the sources listed below, then you'll discover that there are far too many sweepstakes to enter them all. When I win a big prize, someone always asks where I heard about the sweepstakes. After winning a Caribbean cruise, a co-worker seemed almost green with envy and nearly demanded to know where I'd found out about the sweepstakes. When I told him that I entered at a grocery store that he goes to nearly every week, he was shocked that he'd missed it. "I've got sweepstakes radar," I explained. "I notice sweepstakes that other people miss."

My "radar" is actually just a simple matter of knowing where to look.

Computers and Winning

The Internet offers contests and sweepstakes of all shapes and sizes, and the majority of these are on the up and up. Utilizing sites that contain search engines, such as Yahoo, Excite, or Lycos, you can quickly access hundreds of web sites that contain valuable information on sweepstakes, lotteries, and contests, as well as personal web pages that can put you in touch with people around the world who share your interests.

Another great benefit to being online is that you can communicate with people throughout the world who share your interest in winning. Online communities are popping up everywhere, and you can bet that for every hobby, occupation, and subject of interest, there are at least a few of these communities. In some cases, membership reaches hundreds of people who can prove to be a helpful resource for beginning as well as advanced sweepstakers.

Organized sweepstaking is catching on fast on the world wide web. More than a few sites exist, and those sites offer a wealth of information and opportunities. And with the popularity of the Internet growing rapidly, you can bet that more sites are on the way. While I was surfing the Net, I found the following sites: www.sweepstakesonline.com and www.sweepthenet.com.

Sweepstakes Online (www.sweepstakesonline.com)

How do online sweepstakes differ from standard mail-in sweepstakes? Well, for the most part, online sweepstakes have the same rules as standard sweeps, and as with standard sweepstakes, you should read all of the rules and regulations very carefully. The main difference between standard and online sweepstakes is the ability to e-mail your entry rather than using conventional mail. As you can imagine, this saves you quite a bit on postage and time. With e-mails, you can simply cut and paste the required information into a new e-mail with a few short keystrokes. No more tired hands from filling out notecards or decorating envelopes! Unfortunately, companies do not want an utter barrage of e-mail, so the entry restrictions tend to be a little more strict in online sweepstakes. Aside from these entry restrictions, there are few differences between standard and online sweepstakes, and some of the online sweeps even have alternate addresses for conventional mail entries. Again, be sure to read each sweepstakes' rules carefully to prevent disqualification.

www.sweepstakesonline.com is a comprehensive sweepstaking site that includes updates on new sweepstakes and contests, winner's lists, stories from entrants and winners, frequently asked questions, and even an area for trading and selling sweepstakes and contest winnings. The site offers a lot for both the beginner and seasoned sweepstaker. It is easily navigable, and you can sign up to receive updates by e-mail.

Sweep the Net Sweepstakes Newsletter (www.sweepthenet.com)

At first glance, this appears to be an online sweepstakes and contest newsletter, but it is so much more than that. This site also offers areas where users can find information on companies that need survey participants and who are willing to reward those participants with prizes. They also have an area entitled "Freebies" that alerts users to sites where free items are offered.

A word of caution is due at this point: you should keep in mind that, in most cases, these companies may be asking for personal information. The same rules apply for Internet sweepstakes and contests that do for any such situation. Regarding personal information and "paying to play," do not give out any information that can be used by illegitimate companies to take your money. This includes credit card and bank account numbers. Also, by giving companies your personal information, either in the form of an online entry or by taking a survey, you may be asking for SPAM e-mail. SPAM is the online equivalent of junk mail and can be very frustrating if received in large amounts. Most web sites have an e-mail address where you can send correspondence. Feel free to send an e-mail asking the company what they do with the information. Do they use it themselves, or do they sell the information to other companies? It is your right to know what will happen to your information. Do not hesitate to ask if you have any questions.

And, as in any situation, use your best judgment. If you have questions about contests or sweepstakes that you find, consult the online community through e-mail. Both sweepthenet.com and sweepstakesonline.com have contact e-mail addresses that you can write to. If you think a certain contest or sweepstakes may not be on the up and up, send out a quick e-mail.

Magazines

The first place you should check for sweepstakes each week is in newspapers and magazines. The most effective medium in which to advertise today is certainly television, but many companies can't afford to advertise all of their promotions on TV due to the high cost of airtime. As a result, they advertise heavily in newspapers and magazines, where ad space is much cheaper. National magazines such as *Reader's Digest* are veritable gold mines for sweepstakes.

If you're planning to be a serious sweepstaker, then you've got to subscribe to at least one national magazine. You may want to try subscribing to several, but you might find that exactly the same promotions are advertised in each. Other magazines that frequently contain advertisements for promotions are *TV Guide, Family Circle*, and *Ladies' Home Journal.* Remember, although companies can't force you to buy anything in order to enter a sweepstakes, they certainly hope that you will buy their products. That's the reason sweepstakes exist at all.

As a result, companies try to advertise in magazines that are read by the people whom they think will buy their products. Moreover, the prizes given away in sweepstakes sometimes reflect the kind of products that the company sells. Therefore, if you're interested in winning a car or other automotive products, then you might want to flip through a car magazine every now and then. If you want a house or home furnishings, then take a look at several home decorating magazines. You might even find it possible to combine two separate hobbies in this way, which could be a very rewarding experience.

Since subscribing to magazines can become expensive, you might want to take regular trips to the local library. In consideration of everyone else, you shouldn't rip out any entry forms that you find in magazines or newspapers there, but you can at least photocopy the forms or write down the addresses and complete rules for each sweepstakes. If you're creative, you'll be able to think of even more places to find magazines. Just last week, I was flipping through a friend's latest *Smithsonian* magazine and found a sweepstakes that was sponsored by a dog food company. The prize was a brand-new BMW. Now, I would argue that the typical *Smithsonian* reader is not the type to sit down and create a lot of entries for the sweepstakes, and so the offer was that much more exciting.

This also illustrates an important point regarding where to look for sweepstakes and contests: Don't limit yourself! There are hundreds of periodicals out there, and to attract new customers, companies will try out new or different publications. This can work to your advantage, and you should at least skim through some of the more unsweepstakes-like publications.

What about while you're waiting in your dentist's office? Or at your friends' houses? Garage sales? Thrift stores? Don't limit yourself to national magazines. Although there are cases of fraud in sweepstakes advertised in local newspapers and magazines, most of them are still very legitimate. And if you like the prizes that some of them offer, don't be afraid to enter them. The most you might lose is five minutes of your time, a piece of paper (or two), an envelope, and a postage stamp.

I also survey my local paper every day, and it's turned out to be one of my best sources of sweepstakes information. I look for announcements of grand openings or special sales events, which often include some sort of giveaway to lure customers into the store. And you might find, as I have, that the coupon section of your Sunday paper is also a treasure trove of sweepstakes announcements.

Sweepstakes and Lottery Newsletters

One of the best sources for information on both upcoming sweepstakes and lottery tips is the growing number of newsletters devoted exclusively to help sweepstakers and contesters. Not only do such newsletters provide information on sweepstakes, but they usually contain inspiring stories of the latest big winners. I've gotten great advice from many of them and have also heard of dozens of sweepstakes that would have otherwise passed me by. I advise that if you can afford it, you should subscribe to one or more. Here's a list of some of the more popular newsletters in the country:

Best Sweepstakes
  Newsletter
P.O. Box 421163
Plymouth, MN 55442

Contest News-Letter
P.O. Box 58637
Boulder, CO 80322-8637

Contest News-Letter
  Deluxe
P.O. Box 58637
Boulder, CO 80322-8637

Cooking Contest Chronicle
Karen Martis
P.O. Box 10792
Merrillville, IN 46411-0792
(219) 887-6983

Dreamers Newsletter
P.O. Box 1244
Naugatuck, CT 06770

Granny's Gossip Gazette
P.O. Box 1394
Chula Vista, CA 91912

Jackpotunities
Box 393
Centuck Station
Yonkers, NY 10710
(914) 664-5242
(914) 723-6427

Liz's Sweeps
P.O. Box 356
Norma, NJ 08347

Lottery Player's
  Magazine
321 New Albany Road
Moorestown, NJ 08057
(609) 778-8900

Prize Newsletter
16748-C E Smokey Hill
Road, #29
Aurora, CO 80015

Sweepstakes Profiles
P.O. Box 308
Buckner, KY 40010

Sweepstakes: The Inside
  Scoop
2028 Champions Drive
La Place, LA 70068
(504) 652-7580

The Winners List
P.O. Box 606
Hope Mills, NC
  28348-0606

Winning!
Subscription Service
  Center
P.O. Box 55553
Boulder, CO 80322
(918) 366-4441

Winning Sweepstakes
  Newsletter
Sebell Publishing Co., Inc
P.O. Box 1468
Framingham, MA 01701
(508) 820-1800

You might also consider attending a sweepstakes convention. They are held annually in exciting destinations, and fellow sweepstakers get a great opportunity to socialize, share ideas, listen to guest speakers and win prizes. Information about upcoming conventions is available in most reputable sweepstakes newsletters and related web sites. For those of you who are interested in the conventions but are unable to attend, videotapes which feature the major events and meetings are usually available for purchase.

Local Shops

The next place you should always look is in supermarkets and other local shops. Since many companies that run sweepstakes make products found in local stores, it's only natural that they should advertise their promotions in these retail outlets. It's usually very easy to find sweepstakes notices, as well as their entry forms, in stores. Most companies specifically ask shop managers to place them in a location that is likely to be seen by customers. Most often they can be found on the shelves right next to the products that the company sells. They're also usually located near the checkout stands, where people are liable to take note of them while waiting to pay for their goods. Occasionally, some stores have special bulletin boards where you can find notices for promotions. You may wish to ask the store manager about such a board.

If you can't find any entry forms alongside the sweepstakes notices, don't hesitate to ask the store manager about them. Sometimes experienced sweepstakers have already grabbed all the entry forms, but the managers make sure to keep some extra ones in their office. And sometimes the manager simply forgets to place the entry forms in the storefront. If you absolutely cannot track down any entry forms, then take a few minutes to read the rules on the sweepstakes notice. Perhaps the rules will give an address where you can write for an entry form. Or perhaps, as with most sweepstakes, you can simply enter the promotion with an index card or piece of paper.

Grand openings and store anniversaries are often tied to sweepstakes. It's a good idea to be prepared with a pen in case you happen upon such a promotion. Most people just fill out a form or two and deposit them in the box. But it takes more effort than that to win. I usually take a large stack of forms (always leaving some behind for other sweepstakers, of course) and take them home to fill out. I then feed the forms into the box (or boxes) over the course of the sweepstakes. If there are various locations, I try to have a few in each box so that when they mix the boxes together, my forms will be scattered evenly throughout the larger container. I also wait until the last day and put in a number of forms to insure that at least a few of my forms will be on the very top. Using this method, I once walked away with a trip to Puerto Rico, three color TVs, and a $100 gift certificate. In short, it was worth the effort.

Sweepstakes and Contest Clubs

Your next option for locating sweepstakes is probably the most enjoyable, but it certainly requires the most time. Many experienced sweepstakers across the country are forming sweepstakes and contest clubs. These clubs are a wonderful way of networking information about promotions. You can share information and entry forms with your friends. By joining such a club, you not only limit the amount of work you have to do (rather than check every grocery store in town, you only have to check one, because other people in the club are responsible for other stores), but you can also build some lasting friendships. Some of these clubs have grown to such large memberships that they now actually hold national conventions.

The clubs offer the opportunity to swap not only ideas but prizes as well. It's both a great thrill and a huge morale booster when one of your fellow members wins a grand prize, as often happens. Since most trip prizes are usually good for two people, you might be invited by (or invite) a fellow member on your vacation.

Here's a list of just a few of the regional sweepstakes and contest clubs in your area. I've tried to include a club for every region in the country. If you send in a self-addressed stamped envelope asking for information, they'll send you material about their club, or be able to refer you to the club nearest you. If there's no such club in your area, you can take the initiative and organize one yourself. I think you'll be surprised at how many friends and neighbors will warm to the idea of joining!

The Cactus Clan
Helene Rosdhal
P.O. Box 83526
Phoenix, AZ 8507

Arkansas State
 Contesters
ViAnn Heat
Rt. 1, Box 133LL
Cabot, AR 72033

San Diego Sweepers
Mary Kelly
14773 Penaquitos Dr.
San Diego, CA 92129

California Central Coast
  Sweepers
P.O. Box 1492
Santa Maria, CA 93456

California Winners
R.E. Hale
P.O. Box 11703
Fresno, CA 93774-1703

California Dreamers
David Herrick
21 Bonita Ave.
Piedmont, CA 94611

Orange County
  Sweepstakes Club
Sonia Abrahams
10201 Slaten
Fountain Valley, CA
  92708

Mile-Hi Sweepers
Kathie Parent
767 S. Xenon Ct.
Lakewood, CO 80228

Connecticut Sweeps
  Connection
Jo Tatum
65 Noroton Ave.
Darien, CT 06820

Delaware Diamonds
Sue Matz
614 Berwick Rd.
Wilmington, DE 19803

The Central Florida
  Sweepstakers
e-mail:
  Tahorrocks@aol.com.

Central Florida
  Sweepers
Mickey Eagle
1014 Ibsen Ave.
Orlando, FL 32809

So. FL Treasure Hunters
Martha Monaco
300 NW 82 Ave., #150
Plantation, FL 33324

Miami Sweepstakes Club
Send an SASE to:
8390 West Flagler Street,
  #214
Miami, FL 33144-2039

Winners Circle of
  Southwest Florida
1417 Del Prado
Boulevard, #191
Cape Coral, FL 33990

Macontesters
Eileen Preson
P.O. Box 7763
Macon, GA 31209

Metro Atlanta Winners
Sandra Hight
P.O. Box 10
Stone Mountain, GA
  30086

Iowinians
Tammy Schell
2219 Sunnyside Circle
Cedar Falls, IA 50613

The Tri-State
  Sweepstakers
Phillip Gene Spotts
P.O. Box 431
Decorah, IA 42101-0431

Jan Tilton
40586 Riverview Dr.
Cataldo, ID 83810

Illinois Dream Team
Pat Bogseth
2443 Adams Dr.
Lisle, IL 60532

Indiana Rainbows
Sandy Sowl
P.O. Box 24608
Indianapolis, IN 46224

Hoosier Winners
Rhonda Grable
7912 Butt Rd.
Fort Wayne, IN 46818

The Dixieland Winners
Mark
2028 Champions Drive
La Place, LA 70068

Chesapeake Crabs
Victoria Birkett
2917 So. Court
Annapolis, MD 21401

Wolverine
Bennita Sweeter
5087 W. Church Rd.
Perry, MI 48872

Twin Cities Sweepstakes
  Club
Anne Simpson
P.O. Box 581914
Minneapolis, MN
55458-1914

Montana Orediggers
Jan Stowe
Box 2074
Great Falls, MT 59403

Northern New England
  Sweepers
Marion Gagnon
15 Laurel Lane
Somerswoth, NH 03878

New Mexico Sweepers
Joan Brown
8200 Montgomery NE,
#261
Albuquerque, NM 87109

Atlantic City
  Sweepstakers
Michael Goldberg
151 Dickie Ave.
Staten Island, NY 10314

Sin City Sweepers
Lori Franklin
3507 Victory Ave.
Las Vegas, NV 89121

The Queen City
  Sweepstaker's Clubs
QCSC
P.O. Box 3133
Cincinnati, OH
45201-3133

Northwest Sweepers Club
Tammy Lucky
P.O. Box 55261
Portland, OR 97238

Pittsburgh PennPals
Deb Larsen
One Wexford Lane
Pittsburgh, PA 15235

The Greater Memphis
  Sweepers Club
P.O. Box 126
Brunswick, TN 38014-0126

The Bay City Sweepers
Denetra Weaver
4 Sissy Lane
Bay City, TX 77414

Houston Armadillos
Rose Bachman
2926 Plum Creek, #41
Houston, TX 77087

Austin Area Sweepers
Mary Reeves/Joan Val
P.O. Box 3000-237
Georgetown, TX 78628

Texas Rangewriters
John Witmer
6300 Westlake Ave.
Dallas, TX 75214

Northern Virginia
Fortune Seekers
For more information,
contact Cassandra
Burrell at
jupiterx@usa.net or
Diana Caldwell at
lcaldwel@erols.com.
Or send e-mail to
fortuneseekes@juno.com

Capitol Contest Club
Irwin J. Schumacher
2616 Moreland PL. NW
Washington, DC 20015

The Puget Sound Clams
Lorene Palmer
P.O. Box 715
Lake Stevens, WA 98258

The Badger Winners
Muriel Kroening
231 East Park Avenue
Berlin, WI 54923-1637

Technology at Your Grocery Store

Another new development you may already be a part of is the club card, which is offered by many grocery and retail stores. Becoming a member is free and usually only requires that you fill out a form with your name, address, and phone number. You are then given special discounts offered only to club members on specific items that you purchase. In addition to the club savings, you may also be entered into special sweepstakes and giveaways sponsored by the store. You may ask yourself why a store would seemingly give away their profit by passing discounts on to you, the consumer, in exchange for your name, address, and phone number. By keeping track of your purchases, stores and supermarkets are better informed to tailor displays and advertisements to your impulses. While the club discount may be applied to items you normally buy, they also usually apply to items you would not necessarily buy, and these are the discounts that may cause you to switch brands based on cost alone, or to buy items that you wouldn't normally buy. And while the ease of an automatic sweepstakes entry is great, it increases the amount of overall entries in a sweepstakes. Just by using their club card, people can be instantly entered into a sweepstakes that they may have never entered if they had to take the time to fill out an entry form.

Ralph's supermarket, one of the largest grocery chains in southern California, has given away a house, cars, cash, and prizes worth millions of dollars. One of their sweepstakes, known as Dreamstakes 2000, offers one lucky shopper the chance at $2 million.

Where to Find Contests

Now that you know several ways to improve your chances of winning contests, you're probably wondering how to enter them. As with sweepstakes, the three major avenues through which you can find out about contests are magazines, your local stores, and clubs.

If you are interested in recipe contests, then the magazines in which you can find the appropriate entry forms are (naturally) cooking and homemaking magazines such as *Family Circle*. As recipe contests require so much research, it is imperative that you subscribe to one of these magazines, or at least be prepared to make frequent trips to the library. If possible, I would suggest subscribing to two or three magazines, as you will be able to examine a large variety of contests and winning recipes, allowing you to get a good sense of the kinds of dishes that are popular. I realize that this can become somewhat expensive, but it's well worth the cost. Remember, contesting is a hobby that requires some investment.

Many of the word contests are advertised in the same magazines as the recipe contests. This is because many companies that sponsor word contests are food companies. Therefore, if you wish to participate in both types of contests, your financial investment will not necessarily increase.

A good way to lower the cost of such subscriptions is by sharing them with a friend or relative. Perhaps you are interested in word contests, while your brother has a passion for recipe contests. Contesting (and sweepstaking, for that matter) is a hobby that can be shared with your entire family; this will not only reduce the costs of becoming a serious promotions entrant, but it can also be a way to share your time with your loved ones.

As with sweepstakes, most contests are also advertised at your local store. As far as cooking contests go, you will most likely find entry forms in the larger national grocery stores. This is convenient, as these are the stores where you should shop for your ingredients. The entry forms will usually be located near the products that are sponsoring the contest, at the checkout stand, or in the store manager's office. Remember, companies view promotions as a great marketing device, so it should never be very difficult to find the appropriate entry forms. And if you see a contest that you know you want to enter, don't forget to see if you are required to send in some kind of proof of purchase. If you don't already own the product, you might as well save yourself an extra trip by picking one up right then and there. If you enjoy entering both sweepstakes and contests, then you'll probably find yourself being much more selective with the latter, as it can become very expensive to buy products indiscriminately. And, finally, the last place in which you can find out about contests is your local contest club. These clubs are generally even more popular than sweepstakes clubs, as members can actually share skills and practice with each other. In fact, the oldest promotion club in the country is a contest club.

Again, clubs do take a fair amount of time and effort, but they are certainly rewarding. And if you actually enjoy contesting, then there should be no reason for not spending lots of time at it. If there is not already such a club in your town, then you should definitely consider forming one. That way, you can make valuable contacts with whom you can share tips and, hopefully, you can make some friends as well.

If you do decide to form a contest club, then remember that the most important activities you can organize are practice sessions. Each week, when you have club meetings, ask everyone to bring in a practice limerick for the other members to complete. You could establish specific criteria by which the limerick (or any other type of word contest, such as explaining why you use a certain product in 25 words or less) will be judged. After everyone has completed the practice contest, you can decide on a winner and discuss why you felt that entry was the best.

Moreover, if you hold club meetings in someone's house, then you can also practice recipe contests in the kitchen. Each week you can decide upon a specific ingredient around which to center the recipe, and then everyone can try to concoct the best dish possible. By practicing in this fashion, you can assure yourself of the ability to create quick and easy dishes that anyone can prepare.

If your contest club really starts to blossom, then you could even consider inviting guest speakers, such as previous winners or spokespeople from companies that regularly sponsor contests. By doing this, you can learn valuable winning strategies and techniques. As you can see, a contest club can easily grow very large and offer many activities to improve your skills. Your club could become a very rewarding organization for all of its members.

National Contests

There are three national recipe contests of which you should definitely be aware. The first is the Pillsbury Bake-Off contest. This is the single most famous cooking contest in the country, and you've probably already heard of it, but I'd like to discuss it briefly at this point. The top prize is a cash award of one million dollars, and there are several other generous runner-up cash awards as well. There are four categories in which you can enter (and you can enter as many as you like): Easy Weeknight Meal; Yummy Vegetable; Fast and Fabulous Desserts; and Treats, Casual Snacks, and Appetizers. This is the contest that you must enter each year, as the potential awards are so high. Also, you can now enter the contest online, via the Pillsbury Bake-Off website at www. bakeoff.com

The second is the National Pineapple Cooking Contest, in which semi-finalists are flown to Hawaii in order to prepare their recipes for the judges. Again, the prizes are astronomically generous. And the third is the National Chicken Cooking Contest, in which semifinalists are chosen from each state to compete in a final cook-off against each other. All three of these contests are gala events that you wouldn't want to miss. Be on the lookout for information and entry forms in all the places that have been discussed in this chapter.

In case you're unable to find entry forms at your local shops, here are the addresses for the big three. Just write, with a self-addressed, stamped envelope included, and they'll send you all the information you need to get started:

National Chicken Cooking Contest
National Broiler Council
P.O. Box 28158
Central Station
Washington, DC 20005

National Pineapple Cooking Contest
Pineapple Growers Association of Hawaii
c/o Allen and Dorward, Inc.
747 Front Street
San Francisco, CA 94111

The Pillsbury Company
2866 Pillsbury Center
Minneapolis, MN 55402
Phone: (800) 767-4466
Web site: www.bakeoff.co

Cooking Contest Central is a wonderful resource for all types of cooking contests, tips for winning, cookbooks and reviews, and a wealth of other contest and cooking-related information. When you visit their site, don't forget to sign up for free e-mail notification of new contests. You can find them at www.recipecontests.com.

One of the most useful sections of the web site deals with ongoing cooking contests. I have included a section from their web site below, but for up-to-the-minute accuracy, visit. And, as you know, the contests, prizes, and deadlines are subject to change.

California Tomato Commission
Monthly drawing from recipe entries using tomatoes.
Deadline: Monthly
Prizes: T-shirts or visor. All entries get a refrigerator
  magnet and set of recipe cards.
Website:
  http://www.tomato.org/tips-pgs/contest.htm
Mail to:
California Tomato Recipe Contest
1625 E. Shaw Ave. #122
Fresno, Calif. 93710

Canola Oil Recipe Contest
Enter an original recipe that uses canola oil that
  will be judged by a nutritionist. Enter as many
  times as you wish.
Deadline: End of each month
Prizes: Oven mitts and apron, cookbook and T-shirt
  or golf shirt
Website:
  http://www.canola-council.org/nutritin/contest.html

Christopher Ranch Garlic

Monthly contest using garlic.

Deadline: Ongoing

Prizes: Caps, t-shirts, gift packs or garlic braids

Website: http://www.internets.com/garlic/website8.htm

Mail to:

Christopher Ranch

Attn: Recipe Contest

305 Bloomfield Ave.

Gilroy, CA., 95020

Claude's Sauces

Submit a recipe using one of Claude's sauces.

Deadline: Ongoing

Prizes: $50, plus a t-shirt and a set of recipe cards

Website:
  http://www.claudessauces.com/cld_recipcontest.htm

MORE INFO: recipes@claudessauces.com

Cooking Light

Submit a light recipe using Claude's.

Deadline: Ongoing

Prizes: A case of your favorite Claude's product

Website: http://cookinglight.com/inside/events/50bucks.html

Mail to:

Reader Recipes

P.O. Box 1748

Birmingham, Ala. 35201

Fish Master Seafood Recipe Contest

An original recipe for any seafood is drawn at random.

Deadline: Monthly

Prizes: Seafood selection of the month

Website: http://www.fishmaster.com/contest.htm

Granny's Coupons
Weekly recipe winners in all categories.
Deadline: Ongoing
Prizes: $20
Website:
  http://www.grannys-coupons.com/recipes/enter.html
Mail to:
Granny's Recipes
10225 Kill Creek Road
DeSoto, Kan. 66018.

Honeysuckle White Turkey
Several categories to choose from for your turkey recipe.
Deadline: Ongoing
Prizes: $100
Website:
  http://www.honeysucklewhite.com/recipes/recipetoc.html
Mail to:
Honeysuckle White
Consumer Recipe
P. O. Box 225
Springdale, Ariz. 72765

Jolly Time Popcorn
Your favorite popcorn recipe can win a prize.
Deadline: Ongoing
Prizes: Jolly Time Popcorn apron
Website: http://www.jollytime.com/prizes.html

Kokopelli Herbs Recipe Contest
Must use one of the Kokopelli herb blend products.
Deadline: Monthly
Prizes: 1/4 pound of a Kokopelli herb blend
Website: http://www.gj.net/~sheldave/contest.htm

Lighthouse Monthly Recipe Contest
Must use Lighthouse salad dressing as an ingredient.
Deadline: Monthly
Prizes: Lighthouse apron or tote bag
Website: http://www.litehousefoods.com/contest.html

Mountain Gourmet
Send in your favorite recipe for monthly prizes.
Deadline: Ongoing
Prizes: A cherry wood Shaker oval dressing tray or
   cooling rack.
Website:
   http://www.mountaingourmet.com/recipe/contest.html

There are other well-respected national contests that you'll read about when doing your research in magazines and grocery stores, but you should also remember that local organizations, religious groups, and schools often hold recipe contests. While you obviously won't win huge cash awards from these smaller promotions, you might win some nice prizes, and you can definitely practice your skills.

Contests for the Whole Family

One of the more rewarding aspects of entering contests is that, unlike sweepstakes, you can make it something of a family affair. Not only can you get your kids to help with slogans and recipes, but you can also assist them in entering contests of their own.

A growing number of organizations and companies have established contests for children and young adults. Many of the contests are not only potentially lucrative, but are also educational—from essay and photography contests to science Olympiads. And, of course, there's also the world-famous Scripps Howard spelling bee that gets national attention every year. In fact, the range of contests for kids is as large or larger than for their parents. Such contests give kids fun rainy-day projects and teaches them the discipline and pleasure of competition. And it's a hobby you can share with your kids, rather than just sitting around watching television.

Prizes for such contests range from savings bonds to college scholarships to fun-filled family vacations. Often, the prize consists of having your child's name appear over his or her short story or artwork. Such recognition does wonders for a child's growing sense of self-esteem. And even if the child doesn't win first prize in a contest, chances are good that they'll learn something along the way.

As with their adult counterparts, there are always rules to follow to ensure success in children's contests. Make sure your child understands what's expected, whether it be a drawing or photograph, and that they use the proper form before sending in their entry. Be neat, punctual, and to the point. If there's an entry fee (which there often is), make sure that you're comfortable with it. As with lotteries, don't spend more on an entry fee than you'd mind losing.

Also, be sure that the competition will be enjoyable for your child. A 15-page essay on molecules or construction of a model of the Eiffel Tower might end up being more of an ordeal than you or your child would want. The whole point, as with sweepstaking, is to have fun. Winning is not as important as striving for quality. Try to get your kids to enter contests that feature activities they already like. If your child doesn't like poetry, it's not going to be much fun to enter a poetry contest. Maybe they prefer entering a contest for best watercolor painting or figuring out riddles or playing the piano. You probably already know what kind of materials—clay, wood, fabric—your child prefers to play with. This is an indication of the types of contests they should enter. Don't think so much about the prize; rather, think about what your child will learn along the way.

The range of contests for kids is really vast. If your child raises hamsters, for example, there might be a local 4-H contest in your area where they can show off their prize animals. Check into local clubs for kids, such as the Boy's Club, 4-H, or Girl Scouts to see what types of contests they hold for members. And also research local coloring contests if your kids show an interest in art.

Here are just a few of the hundreds of annual contests for kids. I've included addresses you can write to for more information, but make sure to include a self-addressed stamped envelope to make sure they get back to you. You can also check with your child's school, as well as the many magazines geared toward kids:

Annual National PTA
  Reflections Theme
  Program
Visual Arts Category
National P.T.A.
700 North Rush Street
Chicago, IL 60611-2571

Music Awards to Student
  Composers
Broadcast Music, Inc.,
320 West 57th St.
New York, NY 10019

Sew 'N Show Contest
The McCall Pattern
  Company
230 Park Avenue, Room
  1038
New York, NY 10163

National Computer Art
  Competition
West Educational
  Publishing
Computer Art Contest
201 Castro Street, 4th floor
Mountain View, CA 94041

All-American Soap Box
  Derby
P.O. Box 7233
Derby Downs
Akron, OH 44306

National Model Airplane
  Championships
Academy of Model
  Aeronautics
1810 Samuel Morse Drive
Reston, VA 22090

INVENT AMERICA!
  Contest
United States Patent
  Model Foundation
1331 Pennsylvania
Avenue, NW, Suite 903
Washington, DC 20004

Scripps Howard National
  Spelling Bee
P.O. Box 371541
Pittsburgh, PA 15251-7541

Jumping Frog Jubilee
Calaveras County Fair
P.O. Box 96
Angels Camp, CA 95222

Young Writer's Contest
Young Writer's Contest
  Foundation
P.O. Box 6092
McLean, VA 22106

Science Olympiad
5955 Little Pine Lane
Rochester, MI 48064

Young American
Horticulture Contests
National Junior
  Horticultural Association
1847 Hess Lake Drive
Newaygo, MI 49337

MADD (Mothers Against
  Drunk Driving)
Poster Contest
MADD
699 Airport Freeway,
Suite 310
Hurst, TX 76053

The Scripps Spelling Bee is the nation's largest and longest-running educational promotion, administered on a not-for-profit basis by The E.W. Scripps Company and 239 sponsors throughout the world. In general, the program is open to students who have not reached their 16th birthday on or before the date of the national finals and who have not passed beyond the 8th grade at the time of their school finals. You can mail the E.W. Scripps company for more information on eligibility and sponsorships at:

Scripps Howard National Spelling Bee
P.O. Box 371541
Pittsburgh, PA 15251-7541

CHAPTER 8

How to Become a Game Show Contestant

I'D LIKE YOU TO CONSIDER another path toward your dream of winning cash, cars, and trips. It may take more effort on your part, but could end up as a memorable—and profitable—experience.

I'm talking about being a game show contestant, as in "I'd like to buy a vowel, Pat" or "Offbeat Museums for $500, Alex!" Although getting on such a show may seem like a remote possibility, people just like you end up on television every day. In fact, the odds of winning $25,000 on "Wheel of Fortune" are much greater than hitting it big in a lottery. It's also more likely that you'll end up on the panel of "Jeopardy!" than winning Publisher's Clearing House.

That's the good news. The not-so-good news is that getting to be a contestant on most game shows does require a fair amount of work on your part. Still, haven't we all watched game shows and thought to ourselves, "I could do better than her!" Haven't you ever had the answer faster than a contestant on "Jeopardy!"?

Game shows have always been popular with viewers. And, in an attempt to capitalize on this popularity, the Game Show Network has been devoted solely to game shows. On this channel, you can watch game shows from the dawn of television back to back with current game shows. Some of the new shows allow viewers to call into the studio and play along with the contestants, and a web page on the world wide web will provide you with all of the shows available and their airtimes. Visit the Game Show Network site on the web at www.spe.sony.com/gsn.

For those of you who want to be in the limelight, game shows are a healthy supplement to sweepstakes and contests. The first week I moved to Los Angeles, I used the techniques I'm about to tell you about to get on "The Match Game" with Gene Rayburn. Between smiling a lot, being well-dressed, and knowing the game, I took home $6,000. That got me hooked on winning, and I haven't looked back since then. To date, I have been a contestant on five game shows with wins in cash and prizes totaling over $25,000.

At one time there were fewer restrictions with regard to the number of game shows a person could be on and it was not uncommon to see many of the same contestants showing up on numerous shows. Now there are legal limits that shows must abide by. Currently, restrictions can vary depending on the show but generally contestants must wait at least one year between game show appearances. Some shows stipulate that you can only be on 3 shows in a 10-year period. Cable game show restrictions can be less strict; however, they usually require you wait at least a year between shows. When you audition you will be asked about previous game show appearances and air-dates.

Game Show Myths

Let me start by dispelling a few myths that swirl around game shows. First off, no, you don't have to look like Mel Gibson or Michelle Pfeiffer to get on a game show. People often think that they're not glamorous enough, when in fact just the opposite is true. Game show producers want contestants that the average American can relate to. That means that being too good-looking will probably work against you when it comes to game shows. Producers want variety as well—all races and ages, male and female—so you have as good a chance as anyone else.

Another misconception about game shows is that you have to be a college professor or lawyer to play. Sure, on "Jeopardy!" you have to be able to handle some pretty advanced questions, but that's the exception rather than the rule. You don't have to be a brain surgeon to get on "Wheel of Fortune." Many people feel that they would simply be too nervous to appear before the television cameras and, in some cases, live audiences. Sure, having to perform like that will be a bit nerve-wracking. But, as you'll read in a minute, you can go a long way to overcoming the jitters by knowing the game as well as possible and rehearsing it with friends and family.

So even if you're nervous about game shows, even if you don't look like a movie star, you have as good a chance as anyone of getting on. Here's why: What the producers want more than anything are people who know how to show their good sides, who know how to smile and display emotions. Most importantly, they want people who know how to be themselves. That's you, isn't it? Besides, it's only a game show. The worst that can happen is you don't get picked but have an interesting experience to tell your friends about. And, if you get on the show but end up losing, you could get consolation prizes worth up to several thousand dollars. So what's to be nervous about? Don't worry too much about living far away from Los Angeles, where most game shows are produced. Number one, more and more game shows are now being produced locally in places like Chicago and San Francisco. As more and more cable stations come on line, there will be more and more local game shows to go along with them. So even if you must travel, the distance might not be too great. Also, big game shows such as "Wheel of Fortune" hold auditions regularly in cities across the country, which saves you the expense of traveling to California.

Choosing a Show That's Right for You

Before you get started on your journey to become a game show contestant, watch a variety of shows and pick the one you think might be right for you. See what kinds of prizes they give away and what kinds of questions they ask. A good way of determining what kinds of game shows you might do well on is simply to look at the types of games you like to play at home. Do you enjoy Scrabble? Trivial Pursuit? Crossword puzzles? Do you have any special areas of interest, like music or history? If so, you might be able to pick a game show that can utilize your talents. Since most of us have grown up watching game shows, many people already have an idea of what show suits them best.

Once you decide on a game or games that feel right, see if there's a board game version of the show. Play it a few times with friends to make sure you feel comfortable with the format and, of course, enjoy the game.

The best tip I can give for securing a place on a game show is to try out for a brand-new show before it's even aired. They won't have a back record of viable contestants to call, so it will be much easier to get selected. You might not be familiar with the rules of the game but neither will anyone else. As you'll see in a minute, the best place to find out about such new shows is the Classified section in the Sunday edition of the *Los Angeles Times*.

Once you decide on the game you'd like to be on, it's time to get down to real work. First, watch the game endlessly. Use a video recorder so that you can start and stop the game as you please. Study all the nuances of the game, all the rules and regulations. Get a feel for the kinds of questions that are asked and what the host seems to like in a contestant. Which contestants do well? Which don't? If you're watching one of the shows that let the home audience know the answers before the contestants, try to block out the answer so that it's as tough for you as it is for the contestant. Keep playing the board game version until you have it down pat.

Learn the special language used on each game show, such as the way answers must be phrased as questions on "Jeopardy!" As with sweepstakes and contests, make sure to know the rules backwards and forwards. Not knowing the rules and etiquette of the game can get you eliminated from auditions in the first round, so commit them to memory. It's impossible to go into the various rules and regulations here, but once you decide on a show, you should have no trouble deciphering the rules specific to that show.

There are also many computer games of your favorite shows as well, which may come in handy. Check your local computer store to see what's out there. Keep careful track of your progress. If you have the time and inclination, you might even want to write the producer for tickets so you can watch the show being taped. This will give you an intimate feel for what it's like to be on stage, and also further familiarize you with the rules and rhythm of the show. Like the man said when asked how to get to Carnegie Hall, the key is practice, practice, practice!

Depending on the show you've picked, it might be good to start studying up on general knowledge— U.S. history, art, music, etc. I myself have started a small library for use not only for game shows, but other contests as well. You might want to do this yourself. Here are a few of the books I often use:

The Mensa Genius Quiz Book
by Abbe Salny
Addison Wesley Publishing

The Book of Answers
by Barbara Berliner
Prentice Hall

The Complete Unabridged Super Trivia Encyclopedia
by Fred L. Worth
Warner Books

Don't Know Much About History
Don't Know Much About Geography
by Kenneth C. Davis
William Morrow and Company

What's Your Sports IQ: The Unofficial Guide to
Sports Literacy
by Bill Jeakle and Ed Wyatt
Plume Penguin

History's Trickiest Questions
by Paul Kuttner
Dawnwood Press

The World's First Quiz Almanac
by Inese and Frank Gruber
A&W Visual Library

The Random House Book of 1001 Questions and
Answers
by Bridget and Neil Ardley
Random House, New York

80 Great Word Puzzles
by Jacqueline E. Mathews
Ivy Books

The Jeopardy! Challenge
by Alex Trebek and Merv Griffin
HarperCollins

How to Beat the Wheel of Fortune
by William Ryan
Ryan Publishing

Secrets of the Jeopardy! Champions
by Chuck Forrest and Mark Lowenthal
Warner Books

Passing the Audition

So you've picked out the game and have studied it until you're blue in the face. Now it's time to put your new knowledge to use by trying out for the show. How do you find out when and where auditions are being held? I've found that the simplest way is to look on the front page of the Sunday *Los Angeles Times* Classified section. Most of the big game shows give information about upcoming auditions. Don't be alarmed—even if you live in Albuquerque, your local library will probably carry the *L.A. Times.*

You can also write a simple post card to your favorite game show and ask for information about upcoming auditions. In some cases, a phone call may get you all the information you need. (Check the end of this chapter for a list of game shows and their addresses and/or phone numbers). Normally, auditions are open to all comers. Find out from your show the regulations regarding audition sign-ups. See if your show is planning to hold an audition in your area any time soon. If not, you may need to travel to stand a chance of getting on the show—and, unfortunately, this is at your own expense, not the game show's. If this is the case, I recommend combining your audition with a trip to see friends, or a short vacation. If you don't get on the show, then at least you've had a nice time trying. And don't let the fact that you're from a different region of the country stop you from auditioning. As I said, producers want more than anything to represent a cross-section of American life, because that's who makes up their audience. And that's also who buys their sponsor's products. Being from a distant corner of the country will probably be to your advantage.

On the day of audition, wherever it may be, my best piece of advice is this: Relax and don't forget to smile! This is not a job interview or college exam. It's just a game show. If you get on, great. If you don't, you'll still have probably had a good time. Besides, the producers are looking for the kind of people who are composed under pressure. So take a deep breath and keep it all in perspective. Another piece of advice? Don't try to be someone you're not. A savvy producer will see through you in ten seconds. Besides, they're not looking for someone else. They're looking for you!

When you go to a game show audition, you will likely be given some forms to fill out before the actual audition. Most of these forms are standard personal information forms, and you will need to give your name, address, and phone number. The show will want as much information as possible in case they need to get in touch with you in a hurry, which some-times happens when other contestants cannot attend.

In addition, you must sign a waiver that gives the producers permission to use you on television. This waiver is necessary not only for your appearance on the show, but should the producers decide to use your footage in a commercial, you are agreeing to waive all compensation. These are all standard procedures.

You will also be asked some personal information—an interesting tidbit about yourself, be it an accomplishment, hobby, or perhaps even an embarrassing moment. You will also need to list any other game shows that you have been on recently. This information is important because it allows game shows to choose people who are not trying to make a living from game shows. You may also be asked to give your social security number in advance for tax purposes. Should you win cash or prizes on the show, you will be responsible for state and federal taxes on your winnings.

After all of the paperwork comes the actual audition. Auditions vary from show to show, and the format usually depends on the nature of the show. At some point in the audition, you will probably be asked to stand up in front of the group and talk a little bit about yourself. I call this the "Quick Self Speech," and even though this is something that we may have done in other situations in our lives, it never fails to catch some people off guard. Do not be fooled by the simplicity of this task . . . it is an important part of the audition. Remember the old phrase, "You never get a second chance to make a first impression." This is especially true at auditions. These quick speeches give the contestant coordinator and producers the first glimpse of your personality and shows how well you present yourself in front of a group. It is a good idea to have a small speech prepared in advance, so you don't stumble through your words. Of course, you also don't want to have something so well rehearsed that it appears canned or lifeless. Many people's speeches end up sounding like a military recital of their name, rank, and serial number! This is almost as bad as not being prepared at all.

At my first game show audition, for "Match Game," I had nothing prepared to say. For some reason, when it was my turn to speak, I said that I was getting married in Times Square in New York City on New Year's Eve, when the great glowing ball drops. Luckily, this fabrication caught the attention of the group as well as the producers. One lady in the group even blurted out that I was much too young to be getting married and maybe I should reconsider.

Now, I am not recommending that you fictionalize your life for the purpose of successfully getting through a game show audition, but if you're stuck, you might as well come up with something interesting! Just don't make it too outrageous. No producer wants a pathological liar on his or her show. If you have an unusual career, use it to your advantage. If you have an interesting hobby, use it to your advantage. Do not, I repeat, do not give your whole life story. If you stand up and begin with "I was born in room 313 at Madison General Hospital . . .," you might as well start passing out the pillows. Keep your speeches short and upbeat. Practice if you have to, but keep some amount of spontaneity. When it is your turn, stand up straight, smile, be yourself, speak loudly and clearly, and have fun!

The next step might be a written test to determine your knowledge and ability to play the game. For example on the test for "Hollywood Squares" you are given a list of trivia statements. You then select if you agree or disagree with each statement. In order to pass the first stage of auditions for this show you have must answer a predetermined amount of statements correctly.

Another important tip I have for those of you that are interested in game shows involves the other players. If you are selected for the show, you will probably be asked to show up early for the taping. The other contestants will be there early as well, and some of them may try a tactic that is effective in intimidating other players, especially those contestants who haven't ever been on a game show before. I call it the "psyche out," and it consists of one seasoned game show contestant promoting his or herself to discourage other players.

I was on one game show where one of the contestants was bragging that she had been on lots of game shows and had won on each show. She went on to brag about a television show producing a story about her and the unblemished winning streak. When it came time to play the game, the other two contestants that she had been bragging to froze up when it came time to press their buzzers and answer the questions. Guess what? The bragging lady racked up another win. Now, there may be other reasons why the two other contestants froze up, but I have seen the psyche out on many other occasions, and it almost always has the same effect.

You may also encounter hard feelings from other contestants. I have found that the best reaction is to just smile and ignore them. If you let their unsportsmanlike conduct distract you, you will not be in top shape for the rest of the game. On one game show, a contestant that I had beaten huffed and puffed and did everything but snarl outright at me as I was going onstage to meet my next challenger. I just smiled and went out to play the next round. Which I promptly won!

Being on a game show is a lot like entering a beauty contest. No, you don't have to be beautiful. But you do have to remember to smile, smile, smile. Not just a grin, mind you, but a big smile that really shows off your molars. The more the better. I can't overstress the importance of a good smile.

If you make it past the initial stage (and I'm sure you will), you'll finally get to use all that hard work when you participate in a practice run of the show. This is where everything should come together. Take a few deep breaths, relax, and smile. Game show producers also like to see big emotions—not phony, mind you, but big. If you win a prize in the mock game, then give a big reaction. If you miss a question, react with a smile and a self-effacing nod of the head. But don't confuse big emotions with having to act. You should be yourself, but just don't be afraid to show the producer what you're feeling. As George Burns says, "Sincerity is the most important thing of all. And if you can fake that, you've got it made."

If you don't make it past the mockup, then at least you've gained some valuable experience for your next attempt. But let's say you do make the final cut and arrive at the studio for taping. Even though there might be more lights this time, along with a celebrity host and perhaps a live audience, all the same rules apply: despite the increase in pressure, remember to relax, be charming, and show your teeth. Listen closely to whatever instructions that the production assistants might offer—where to stand, when to move, when to stay still, etc. Usually, five shows are taped in a single day, so you may be asked to bring several changes of clothes so you can change between shows if you win.

On the day of taping, you will be given a complete set of rules for the show. Sometimes, the contestant coordinator or an associate producer will go over these rules with you in detail before taping begins. They will instruct you not to speak to any unauthorized people while on set; this helps to ensure that cheating does not occur or that contestants are not favored or given the answers in advance. Certain shows may have a representative from a department called Standards and Practices. It is their job to make sure that contestants are not being given the answers beforehand and that no cheating occurs. You may have seen the movie *Quiz Show,* which explores the game show cheating scandal in the early days of television. Nowadays, great effort is made to ensure a fair game. As a contestant, you must follow the rules to the letter or you will be disqualified.

When the show finally begins taping, when the music comes up, or the studio audience starts to applaud, remember to stay as cordial and calm as you can. No one can help you now, but you've worked long and hard for this moment. You know this game backwards and forwards, and now it's time to strut your stuff. At this point, the worst that can happen is that you get some great consolation prizes. But there's also the very good chance that you'll win big prizes—a new car, thousands in cash, a speed boat . . . All you have to do is remember to smile.

Here's a list of some of the game shows currently in production at the time of publication. If any of them appeal to you, call for information or drop a quick postcard in the mail. Also, check your local cable franchise for a listing of any new game shows in your area:

Change of Heart
3500 West Olive Avenue
#1000
Burbank, CA 91505

Game Show Network
P.O. Box 805
Culver City, CA
90232-0805
(310) 364-2060

Hollywood Squares
Quickstead Productions
7800 Beverly Boulevard
Los Angeles, CA 90076
(323) 850-0707

Jeopardy!
Merv Griffin Productions
10202 West Washington
  Blvd.
Culver City, CA 90232
(310) 280-5367

Love Connection
Pel Productions
4201 Wilshire Boulevard
#610
Los Angeles, CA 90010

The Price is Right
Mark Goodson
Productions
5757 Wilshire Blvd.
Suite 206
Los Angeles, CA
90036-5806
(323) 965-6500 or in NY
(212) 755-3383

Wheel of Fortune
Send a post card with
  your name, address,
  phone number and
  nearest major city to:
Wheel of Fortune
10202 West Washington
Blvd., #5300
Culver City, CA 90232

Where in the World Is
  Carmen Sandiego?
WGBH Television
125 Western Ave.
Boston, MA 02134
(617) 492-2777

Win Ben Stein's Money
Valley Crest Productions
2400 West Alameda Avenue
Burbank, CA 91521-0164

Whose Line Is It Anyway?
Riverside Productions
1438 North Gower Street
Box 27
Hollywood, CA 90028

CHAPTER 9

You're a Winner! Now What?

SO YOU'VE GATHERED THE necessary supplies, read the rules thoroughly, entered every sweepstakes or contest you could find, increased the odds of winning that lottery, searched the aisles of supermarkets, practiced your rhyming skills, auditioned for game shows, concocted magnificent new recipes, joined clubs, and networked with people who share your passion for promotions. . . . And guess what?

You won!

That's right, you won. All of your efforts actually paid off, and you are the proud possessor of a cash prize or a new car or a boat or even a home in the country. You couldn't be happier. All of your friends come over to congratulate you and pat you on the back. You deserve to be proud of yourself, because you've truly accomplished something special, something that most people only dream about.

But it's not all wine, women (or men), and song. I hate to burst your bubble here, but winning can create its own host of troubles. I myself have never had anything but pleasant experiences from winning, but that's just not the case for everyone. I was listening to a number of big lottery winners describing their experiences, and offering a bit of advice. Here are just a few pieces of advice that were offered to newcomers to the giant lotto club:

- Move to a different location as soon as possible: You'll be deluged with requests from charities, friends who think they're charities, unknown relatives, and various and sundry nut cases.

- With all your bundles of new money, see what you can do about changing your name, phone number, and maybe even your social security number.

- Consider plastic surgery.

Exaggeration? Maybe. But such joking around points out a truth about winning. You'll have to be prepared for a major change in your life. You'll have to be prepared for more attention than you're used to, or will want, especially if you win one of the mega-lottos. The good news is that a $20 million win barely causes a ripple in the news media anymore. At least in the more populous states, it now takes upwards of $50 million or so before you'll get the kind of life-altering scrutiny that some people have found so alarming. So try, if you can, to win less than $50 million.

And it's not just giant lottos that can drastically alter your lifestyle; even relatively small sweepstakes and contests can lead to unexpected troubles. Take the case of Denise Whitten, a young woman from Winter Haven, Florida, who won an MTV giveaway titled: "I Hate My Miserable Life." First prize included a new car, a new apartment in a different city, help in finding a new job, and $10,000 in cash. The bliss of winning quickly turned sour when co-workers became jealous of Denise's win and started spreading rumors about her. Denise also made the folks at MTV mad when she decided that she really didn't hate her life all that much and wanted to stay in Florida to pursue opportunities locally. All in all, Denise's win was not the most pleasant experience. Other winners have been arrested, even deported, because of the spotlight that often shines on them.

But for every such story of people who've had lousy experiences, there are dozens and dozens of wonderful experiences. Take the older couple whom I heard on a talk show not long ago. They told the interviewer that winning has meant being able to do the kinds of little things they could never do before. One of their favorite hobbies now is to spot a young couple, maybe with children, in a restaurant and buy them dinner anonymously. "It's the little things," they said. "And anonymously is always the best way to give."

The Public Eye

Another consideration with winning, especially sweepstakes and contests, is the sudden lack of anonymity. Most sweepstakes and contests are not only legally required to publish the winners, they want to publicize their event and those that benefited from it. However, the amount of publicity is usually directly related to the level of prestige and the amount of money and prizes involved in the contest or sweepstakes. What this means is that if you don't feel completely comfortable having your win publicized, you can opt for contests and sweepstakes that are not so visible as others. Lotteries are also required to make the names of the winners public. Again, the amount of publicity varies with the amount of money and number of winners for a particular drawing. For instance, 10 people who win 1/10 of $4 million will probably not get their names or pictures in the paper. One person who wins $50 million will be publicized quite a bit more.

If you read the rules and regulations for a sweepstakes or contest, you will undoubtedly find some mention of what is expected of the winner. By entering the contest, you may be agreeing to be the subject of interviews, appear on television, or something that might require extra or undue effort or expense on your part. Treat the Rules and Regulations section as you would any contract—read and understand it completely.

What to Expect After You've Won Your Fortune

Usually, if you've won a big prize in a sweepstakes or contest, an affidavit will be mailed to you from the prize provider or sponsor which you must sign and possibly have notarized. Basically the affidavit is to confirm your eligibility and it may include a liability and public relations release. Failure to return the affidavit by the stipulated deadline can result in the forfeiture of your prize.

Let's back up a bit to that moment when a judge pulls your name from a barrel or decides your jingle is best or six little balls with your numbers roll onto the track. In the case of most sweepstakes and contests, you should expect the good news of your victory to come via certified letter, sometimes after a phone call from the agency handling the promotion. (Having a film crew from Publisher's Clearing House pull up while you're having a coffee and Danish is the exception to the rule).

So what's next? Although most companies have given up sending out a private detective to make sure winners have complied with the rules, it might happen. But there's no need for you to worry as long as you have followed the rules. If you look back to the chapters of this book that dealt with the rules of sweepstakes and contests, then you will remember that they always include a few disclaimers, such as void where prohibited. That's why it's so important for you to never break the rules: you will be caught. If you're 19 years old, and the contest states you must be over 21, then you'll be disqualified, and you will not receive your prize. If your cousin works for the Yummy-Yum Candy Corporation, then don't bother entering any of their contests or sweepstakes, because you will be disqualified. It is the detective agency's responsibility to find these things out, and they are very thorough in their investigations.

By the way, many states now do some investigation of their lottery winners. With a growing number of deadbeat dads who have not paid child support, some states will now deduct any back custody payments from the lottery prize. And if you owe any back state taxes, you might find those deducted from your winnings as well. If you happen to be wanted by the law, or live in the country illegally, you too might find that winning the lottery is not the greatest thing that ever happened to you. Obviously, such problems are the exception rather than the rule. If you have your affairs in order, you shouldn't expect any problems from a big lottery win.

Many people ask why sponsoring companies don't allow their employees, or relatives of their employees, to enter their promotions. The answer to this is simple. Imagine how dubious people would be if even just one of the company's employees won a major prize; no one would believe that the promotions were on the level, and the sponsoring company's credibility would be destroyed. Rather than allow for the possibility of this happening, the companies simply forbid their employees and their families from entering.

Anyway, if you do win, you are going to find yourself at the center of attention for some time. Not only will your friends and family be phoning all day and night to congratulate you, but you may actually be interviewed by television or newspaper reporters. The sponsoring company will almost definitely send representatives to congratulate you and take your photograph. You might even see a huge photo of yourself at the supermarket the next time you go shopping.

All of this can be quite daunting to unsuspecting winners. But if you keep your head, then you can actually enjoy your brief moments of fame. Unfortunately, too many people get nervous when they are barraged by friends, neighbors, and reporters, and they forget how much fun they could be having by receiving all this attention.

If you live in a small town, then it's quite likely that the whole town will know about your victory within a few days. The local newspaper will probably run a story about you. Chances are, you will receive many phone calls from churches, schools, elderly centers, and other local groups asking for donations, particularly if you won a large cash award. I realize that this may seem like an invasion of your privacy, but I would urge you to consider donating at least a small amount to these groups. The only reason they're calling is because they are legitimately short of funding, so why not share some of your good fortune with them? At the very least, you will get a warm and rewarding feeling in your heart. And, if you're careful about selecting which groups you wish to help out, you'll be able to ensure that your donations are tax deductible.

If you live in a large city, then it's unlikely that you'll be the subject of any major newspaper articles, unless you win a really huge promotion or lottery. But you will still find that word of your victory somehow gets out. You may even find your mailbox stuffed with letters from people all over the city, asking you to help them out of their own hard financial times. I can't give you any sound advice on how to deal with these letters, except to say that there are many people who attempt to take advantage of the fortunate. You must make your own decisions about them. In the past, some winners have found it useful to change their phone number to an unlisted number, and some have also gotten P.O. boxes in order to filter out unwanted letters.

If you win one of the large contests or lotteries, then you could very well be interviewed by some of the same magazines that you subscribed to in order to win. And with the recent rise in the popularity of daytime talk shows, there is even a chance you could be on TV. If you win one of the national recipe contests, then your recipe will certainly be published in magazines, and it may even appear on the labels of cans and other products. Your grandmother's prized recipe for spaghetti sauce could end up a household favorite across the country! Keep in mind that none of this is required. Do it only if you feel like it would be fun. No one can force you onto a talk show or in front of a local television audience.

Ironically, many people actually become depressed upon winning a large prize. They feel guilty for their sudden good fortune. While I'm no psychologist, let me assure you that such feelings are completely normal. Don't let them depress you. Remind yourself that you worked hard to win this prize, that it wasn't simply a random accident, and you deserved it. After winning, some people feel empty inside. This is akin to postpartum depression, or the sadness mothers sometimes feel after giving birth. If you spend months, or even years, of your life working toward a goal, and you suddenly feel like you have nothing left to do once that goal is achieved, it's normal to experience a bit of a let-down. The best cure for such depression is to resume your hobby immediately. Just because you've won one promotion, or one big lottery, why should that stop you from entering another? Take the case of the New York man who won over $600,000 in a lottery in 1986. Good luck, right? Four years later, he played a series of numbers that he saw on his kid's shoe, of all places. He bagged his second lottery, this one for $4 million. You think the odds of winning the lottery are slim, try winning two lotteries. The chance of the man winning two lotteries is a staggering two billion to one!

Some big winners have literally found themselves leading normal lives one day and living the life of Hollywood movie stars the next. Fame and fortune has a way of sweeping the unsuspecting away, changing their lives in ways that make them sad, and somehow getting in the way of their happiness. Don't let this happen to you! If you keep your head on your shoulders, then a cash award or other prize could help you live the life of your dreams. If you feel uncomfortable as a minor celebrity, then don't become a minor celebrity. Do only the bare minimum number of interviews and photo sessions. If you enjoy the sudden attention, then bask in it. The point is, don't let your victory control you. As long as you control it, then it should never result in anything but happiness.

The IRS

In general, prize wins over $600 are reported to the IRS by the prize provider or sponsor. The affidavit, mentioned earlier, that you receive will require you to give your social security number for this purpose. It's your responsibility to report your wins when your file your taxes. The value of the item is normally added to regular income and is taxed at the same rate as other income.

I have only heard of one or two promotions in my entire life in which the taxes were paid for by the sponsoring company. This is why you should be at least somewhat selective in deciding which promotions to enter. You should never try to weasel your way out of paying your fair share in taxes, as painful as it may seem to do so, because you could get into a lot of trouble. At the very least you could wind up paying a fine, in which case almost all of your prize money will be taken away from you, and you could even be sent to jail. Is it really worth going to jail in order to avoid paying a few hundred dollars in taxes? But it is understandable that you should want to pay as little as possible. I cannot advise you on how to accomplish that, however, as tax laws are so complicated. The best I can do is tell you to see a reputable tax lawyer or accountant.

If the prize that you win is cash, then you simply have to declare the exact amount in your income taxes. If the prize is merchandise, then things become slightly more complicated. You must declare the fair market value of the item. Fair market value does not mean wholesale or retail value; it means the amount that a seller, not forced to sell, can demand, and a buyer, not forced to buy, will pay.

If you win a home that costs somewhere around $100,000, you cannot "sell" it to your wife for 5 bucks and then pay taxes on this amount. Five dollars is clearly not the fair market value of this home. Fair market value, once the home has been appraised, will no doubt be in the vicinity of $100,000. This is the amount you must declare, whether you decide to sell it or not.

But what happens if you win some really ugly curtains that retail for $2,000? If you try to sell them, and no one is willing to pay more than $300 for them, then the fair market value might turn out to be around $300. While discrepancies this large rarely occur, occasionally people have had trouble selling their prizes for their full value. This is especially true in the case of customized furniture which would have to be reupholstered to fit into anyone else's house, and in the case of "incomplete" prizes, such as a trip to Acapulco that doesn't include the airfare.

Sometimes it is absolutely impossible to find a buyer, and you find yourself stuck with a prize that you really don't want. In this case, the fair market value you declare will be very low. But don't try to get away with declaring the ugly curtains at $10, because the IRS might not agree with you. In a case such as this, it is best for you to consult your tax lawyer or an IRS agent. Such agents understand that fair market value can be difficult to ascertain, and they are usually very willing to help you determine a reasonable amount to declare. At the very least, they'll probably point you in the direction of certain periodicals and catalogs in which you can find the prices of similar items. And remember, you can always refuse any prize that you have won, thereby relieving you of any tax bills.

A reputable sweepstakes or contest (as most of them are) will most likely tell you what you've won and, more importantly, what you haven't won, as in the case of that trip to Acapulco without the means to get there. It is simply in the best interest of the promotion agency to keep their winners as happy as possible. Remember, good public relations is the reason for all of this in the first place. To that end, the agency will want you to want your prize. They'll try to make it clear from the get-go, then, that you'll be flying coach, not first class, or that the Mercedes you just won does not include a car alarm. Agencies will usually try to oblige any reasonable request, such as a desire for a different color Mercedes.

By the way, it's a very nice gesture to send a thank you note to the company that's given you a prize. It makes them feel good about what they've done, and probably encourages them to put on more promotions so that we can win more prizes!

As mentioned, it often occurs that winners just can't afford the prize they've received. Or, more correctly, they can't afford to pay the taxes on the prize. It's common for the agency to try to help out the winner by having the car dealer buy back the car from the winner or awarding cash instead of the prize.

Obviously, you won't run into this problem with lottery winnings. I've never heard of anyone that objects to winning cash—it's very easy to dispose of. But you will need to pay taxes on it as well. The best advice I can give you is to contact a reputable, trustworthy accountant before collecting your prize. If your state has an option to take the prize in a lump sum (at a greatly reduced amount), your accountant might want to advise you to take that offer. The accountant might want to discuss your investment options—from tax-free municipal bonds to certificates of deposits to IRAs—before you pick up your first check. One of the great benefits of winning a state lottery is that many states waive state taxes (see the box on the following page). The federal taxes, which you'll still have to pay, are almost always taken off the top of each yearly installment.

Winning a huge lottery prize brings up any number of obscure tax questions, which are best handled by a top-notch accountant or tax attorney. One of the most common is the question of inheritance taxes for the children of lottery winners. Let's say the winner dies with 10 years of payments totaling a million dollars still due to him. For reasons best explained by a tax expert, the children must pay the entire tax on the million dollars—and all at once. Unlike the winner, the children can't space out the tax payments as the prize money comes in. A good precaution against such a painful tax is for the parents to take out a life insurance policy to cover the cost of the tax in the event they pass away before collecting all their winnings.

State Tax Policies

State	Resident	Non-resident
Arizona	automatic deduction	same
California	exempt from tax	same
Colorado	automatic deduction	same
Connecticut	doesn't have income tax	same
Delaware	exempt from tax	same
Florida	doesn't have income tax	same
Georgia	automatic deduction	same
Idaho	doesn't have income tax	same
Illinois	automatic deduction	same
Indiana	doesn't have income tax	same
Iowa	automatic deduction	same
Kansas	automatic deduction	same
Kentucky	automatic deduction	same
Louisiana	automatic deduction	same
Maine	automatic deduction	no tax
Maryland	automatic deduction	no tax
Massachusetts	automatic deduction	same

Michigan	automatic deduction	same
Minnesota	automatic deduction	same
Missouri	automatic deduction	same
Montana	variable tax, not automatic	same
Nebraska	automatic deduction	same
New Hampshire	exempt from tax	same
New Jersey	exempt from tax	same
New Mexico	automatic deduction	same
New York	automatic deduction	no tax
Ohio	automatic deduction	same
Oregon	exempt from tax	same
Pennsylvania	exempt from tax	same
Rhode Island	exempt from tax	same
South Dakota	doesn't have income tax	same
Texas	exempt from tax	same
Vermont	exempt from tax	same
Virginia	automatic deduction	same
Washington	doesn't have income tax	same
Washington, DC	exempt from tax	same
West Virginia	automatic deduction	same
Wisconsin	automatic deduction	same

Deductions

As with other forms of income, you can make certain deductions on your winnings for lotteries, sweepstakes, and contests. But you can never actually declare a loss. For example, if you can only sell your $2,000 curtains for $300, you may not claim a loss of $1,700. You have gained at least $300 from this promotion, and you must pay the taxes on that gain. But what kinds of deductions can you make?

You can deduct nearly everything that helped you become a winner. You can deduct the cost of postage stamps, paper, pencils, dictionaries, thesauruses, and the subscriptions to magazines. Remember to save all your receipts for your expenses. And, of course, you can deduct the cost of the lottery tickets you purchased before winning the big prize.

You may not, however, deduct the cost of the items you had to buy in order to enter contests, as these items are considered part of your personal expenses. This is yet another reason why you should choose your contests carefully; you don't want to be stuck with a hundred boxes of stale Yummy-Yum cereal when you can't even get a tax break on them.

And, finally, you must remember that you can only make these deductions if you actually win a promotion. If you do not win, you are entitled to no deductions, even if you have spent hundreds of dollars gathering supplies and purchasing products. Remember, a deduction can only be made against a legitimate source of income, and if you don't win, then you receive no income from promotions.

CHAPTER 10

Frequently Asked Questions and Their Answers

IN STUDYING THESE ISSUES for years, I've compiled a list of some of the most commonly asked questions about lotteries, sweepstakes, and contests.

MY WORK SOMETIMES TAKES ME TO CANADA FOR WEEKS ON END. IS THERE A WAY TO GET LOTTERY TICKETS FROM MY HOME STATE WHILE I'M AWAY?

It depends on the lottery regulations of your home state. The answer, however, is usually yes. In most states, you can buy tickets in advance for upcoming lotteries, sometimes up to six months in advance. Let's say you know you'll be out of the country, or state, in a month. Simply go to your vendor and tell them you'd like to buy advanced lottery tickets for that time period. The dealer should be able to sell you tickets. Check to make sure that the lottery tickets have the correct dates on them.

IS IT WORTH MY MONEY TO BUY A LOTTERY COMPUTER PROGRAM?

I'm afraid it's not. Some unscrupulous companies are offering computer programs that are supposed to help you beat the lottery. There are also small lottery "computers" that look like calculators but have much less use. Look at it this way: If the manufacturers of these programs and machines really knew how to beat the lottery with a computer program, do you think they'd be telling the rest of us? I doubt it. You're better off taking your cue from license plates or your kids' birthdays. In short, these programs are nothing more than computer-age scams.

HAS ANYONE EVER RIGGED A LOTTERY?

People have tried, with little success, to beat the incredible security of lottery games. In one case, a group of Pennsylvania lottery employees weighted down the balls used to decide a pick-three game. They succeeded in getting their numbers—6-6-6—to come up. But they were also caught and thrown in jail.

Lottery officials try to anticipate every possible way that the lottery could be fixed and then attempt to correct it. They also change their security measures often to keep would-be criminals off guard.

WHAT'S THE QUICKEST WAY TO FIND OUT WHETHER I'VE WON OR NOT? I DON'T LIKE TO WAIT UNTIL THE NEXT DAY TO READ THE PAPER.

Clearly, the easiest and most efficient way to find out whether you've won or not is to watch, or listen, to the actual lottery drawing. Not only will you know instantaneously whether you've won or not, but you'll have the excitement of watching as your numbers come up (or don't come up, as is often the case). I've found that many people across the country aren't aware of when or how to watch the winning numbers being drawn. Following is a list of broadcast times across the country. Since stations seem to change (and go out of business) quite often, check your local television guide for the proper time and channel to watch. Remember, you can also check lottery results on the world wide web.

Lottery Broadcast Times
(All times given are p.m.)

State	Day of Game	Time	Station
Arizona	WED/SAT	10:00	Varies by town
California	WED/SAT	7:57	Varies
Colorado	WED/SAT	9:59	Varies
Connecticut	TUES/FRI	8:00	WTXX-TV 20
Delaware	TUES/FRI	7:28	WHYY-TV 12
Florida	SAT	11:00	Varies
Georgia	DAILY	6:59	WSB-TV

Idaho	FRI	9:58	Varies
Illinois	M/W/F/S	6:58	WGN-TV 9
Indiana	SAT	6:58	Varies
Iowa	WED/SAT	6:28	Varies
Kansas	WED/SAT	6:28	Varies
Kentucky	WED/SAT	8:00	Varies
Louisiana	DAILY	9:59	Varies
Maine	M/T/W/TH/ F/S	7:59	WPXT-TV
Maryland	SAT	7:55	WNUV-TV 54
Massachusetts	WED/FRI/ SAT	7:58	WHEH-TV 7
Michigan	M/T/W/TH/ F/S	7:28	Varies
Minnesota	DAILY	6:50	Varies
Missouri	WED/SAT	6:58	Varies
Nebraska	WED/SAT	10:00	KETV
New Hamp	M/T/W/TH/ F/S	7:30	WMUR-TV
New Jersey	MON/ THURS	7:56	Varies
New York	M/W/SA/ SU	9:30	WWOR-TV 9
Ohio	MON/SAT	7:29	Varies
Oregon	WED/SAT	7:29	KOIN Ch. 6
Pennsylvania	TUES/WED/ FRI	6:59	Varies
Rhode Island	TUES/SAT	7:29	WPRI Ch.12
South Dakota	WED/SAT	9:59	Varies

Texas	M/T/W/TH/		
	F/S	9:59	Varies
Vermont	FRI	6:58	WCAX Ch.3
Virginia	WED/SAT	10:58	Varies
Washington	WED/SAT	6:59	Varies
Wash, DC	MON/SAT	7:59	WHMM-TV 32
West Virginia	M/T/W/TH/		
	F/S	6:59	WSAZ-TV
Wisconsin	DAILY	10:23	Varies

A FRIEND OF MINE SAYS THAT EVEN LOSING LOTTERY TICKETS CAN BE WORTH MONEY. HOW IS THIS POSSIBLE?

You're friend is correct—sort of. As a means of drawing in more business, some casinos in Atlantic City and Nevada hold drawings using old lottery tickets. The catch, of course, is that you have to go to the casinos to enter. Casino operators, of course, are banking on the chance that once you head into their casino, you won't be able to resist the temptation to blow $20 at the blackjack tables. So you may end up spending quite a bit of dough for these so-called "last chance" drawings. By the way, merchants who sell lottery tickets will occasionally have these drawings, as well, but the prizes are normally rather small. Keep an eye out for them.

I USUALLY JUST GET THE COMPUTER TO PICK MY LOTTO NUMBERS FOR ME, BECAUSE IT'S QUICKER AND I'VE HEARD THE ODDS ARE BETTER. I ALSO HEARD THAT ONCE A COMPUTER HAS ASSIGNED A

QUICK PICK TICKET, THEN NO ONE ELSE CAN GET THOSE NUMBERS UNLESS THEY PICK THEM THEMSELVES. IS THIS TRUE?

Although it sounds logical, this isn't always the case. I've read of a Colorado case in which two winners both received their numbers using quick picks. They had to split the pot. Check with your state lottery to determine whether your quick pick is the one and only such number combination, or if the specific computer program allows for duplicates. By the way, it's much more likely that a ticket based on birthdays will be duplicated. There are, after all, only 365 birthdays and millions of lottery players.

I SAT DOWN AND TRIED TO FIGURE OUT HOW MUCH I SPENT ON LOTTERY TICKETS LAST YEAR. I THINK IT WAS ABOUT $200. AM I BETTING MORE THAN MOST PEOPLE?

You're actually about average—unless you live in Minnesota, which usually ranks last in per capita sales of lottery tickets. As you might expect, the states with the biggest jackpots also have the highest per-capita sales.

I USUALLY GET MY LOTTO TICKETS AT A 7-11 ON THE CORNER. IS THIS WHERE MOST PEOPLE BUY THEIR TICKETS?

Yes. Quickie convenience stores like 7-11 account for almost half of all ticket sales. Since such stores make a nickel on every ticket sold, lottery tickets have become a large percentage of their sales—well over $500 million a year.

I'VE STARTED TO PLAY OUT-OF-STATE LOTTERIES BUT SOMETIMES HAVE A HARD TIME FINDING OUT IF I'VE WON OR NOT. HOW

SHOULD I GO ABOUT IT?

There are a number of ways, including sending to the state lottery for information or going to the library and checking a major newspaper from the state in which you purchased the ticket. The quickest and easiest way is to log on to your online service and visit a web site which posts winning numbers by state. This method is free, and you don't have to leave the comfort of your own home to get accurate, up-to-date information. The most expensive way of finding out is to call a 900-service that's set up to give the latest winning numbers. Although it's not as economical as some ways, I find that it's just more convenient. You can also call the state lottery offices directly, using the list of phone numbers and addresses provided in chapter three.

SOMETIMES I GET TOO BUSY TO GET TO THE STORE TO GET LOTTERY TICKETS. OR I JUST PLAIN FORGET. IS THERE A WAY TO BUY TICKETS WITHOUT HAVING TO GO TO THE STORE EVERY THREE OR FOUR DAYS?

Yes. Almost all states with lotteries have both advanced and subscription purchases.

For advanced ticket sales, just go to your local vendor and ask the clerk for lottery tickets for whatever games you may want in the future. For example, if you want to buy tickets for the next 10 lotteries, just give the clerk the appropriate dates, and they'll print out tickets for those dates. If you're picking your own numbers, just fill out the forms as you normally would, but put the future dates at the top. And check the tickets you receive carefully before leaving the store. In some states, you can buy advance tickets for up to a year in the future. Obviously, with such a system you can do all your shopping at once, which is very popular for people who live far away from their nearest lottery outlets, or for those who live out of state. But remember to check each and every ticket to make sure you've won.

Another popular method is to buy a subscription to a certain set of numbers. You can usually buy a subscription to every single game in your state for up to a year, or for as many weeks as you choose. Unlike advanced sales, however, you need to purchase subscriptions directly from the state lottery office. The state will usually inform you if you've won or not, but I think it's a good idea to still check regularly for winning numbers. The drawback with subscriptions is that you must have a mailing address within the state to play. But such a system is great for people who are unable to leave home due to illness or mobility problems.

IS IT OKAY TO HAVE A FRIEND OF MINE IN ANOTHER STATE BUY TICKETS FOR ME?

If your question is whether or not it's legal, the answer is probably yes. But check with both your home state and the state from which you want to purchase tickets to make sure.

If you're asking whether it's a good idea to get a friend to buy your tickets, the answer is probably not. Let's say a buddy in California buys two tickets. One for you, another for herself. And then let's say your ticket wins. Unless your friend is saintly, chances are good that she'll say it was her ticket that won. As sad as it seems, there are many such stories of winning tickets that result in the end of friendships and lawsuits. But not all of these relationships end badly. On March 20, 1998, Frank Capaci, 67, and his wife, Shirley, 63, made a place for themselves in lottery history, and they did so through a friend. The Streamwood, Illinois, couple sent five dollars for Powerball tickets with their friends John Marnell and Patty Rooney, who drove to Wisconsin to purchase tickets. They won the world's second-largest lottery jackpot Wednesday night. The couple chose the cash option, making them the recipient of the largest cash sum ever paid out. Marnell and Rooney are bar tenders from Bill's on Barlett, a pub and pizza place the Capaci's spend time in. When the bartenders returned with a sealed envelope with the Capaci's name on it, Frank was surprised. He had forgotten he had sent money for the tickets.

I ONCE READ THAT CONTESTS AND SWEEPSTAKES SOMETIMES DISCRIMINATE AGAINST MINORITIES. IS THIS TRUE?

Although it's possible that this may have happened in the past, it is extremely unlikely that it still occurs. Sweepstakes and contests are now strictly regulated by a slew of laws and codes. If a company were ever caught discriminating against certain groups, it would not only face legal penalties, but an onslaught of bad publicity, which would completely negate the purpose of the promotion. In general, I tell people that sweepstakes are fair and unbiased.

BUT WHAT IF I WIN TOO MANY SWEEPSTAKES? CAN I BE BLACK-BALLED FROM FUTURE SWEEPSTAKES?

I'm afraid that winning too many sweepstakes is rarely, if ever, a problem. To answer your question, no, you cannot be booted from a promotion just because you've won in the past. It's against the law, for one thing. And it would also take too much extra effort for the companies to keep track of winners and be on the lookout for their entries. So don't be too worried if you start winning. However, you may be forbidden to play the same sweepstakes again if you become a winner, but there are plenty of other contests and sweepstakes out there to keep you busy.

I KNOW THAT SWEEPSTAKES AND LOTTERIES HAVE BEEN AROUND FOREVER, BUT WHEN DID CONTESTS BECOME SO POPULAR?

As we've seen, lotteries have been popular down through the ages. Contests, which rely more on skill than luck, seem to have gained widespread popularity in the late nineteenth century. This is partly due to the fact that the private lotteries of that age were so corrupt, few people trusted them. Contests seemed to fill a void. They blossomed during the depression, when they became a ray of hope for millions of unemployed Americans. Their popularity has ebbed and flowed since then, largely in response to the prevailing economy of the time. Not surprisingly, their popularity increased again during the country's most recent recession.

CAN I CLAIM MY LOSING LOTTERY TICKETS AS DEDUCTIONS? WHAT ABOUT THE EXPENSE I'VE INCURRED FOR SWEEPSTAKES?

Again, the rules regarding lottery winnings are a bit confusing, but the answer is, maybe. Let's say you've played the lottery for a year without winning a dime, but spent a thousand dollars. You can't claim a deduction based on the loss. But let's say that the thousand tickets you bought earned you a $5,000 lottery. You can then put the thousand dollars in as an itemized deduction, because your winnings exceed your losses. That $5,000 is recognized as a legitimate source of income, so any money you spent earning it is, thus, a legitimate deduction.

The same logic holds true for sweepstakes. Let's say you've spent $500 on postage, envelopes, and other expenses to enter a thousand sweepstakes last year. If you don't win any of them, then you're out the $500. But if you win Publisher's Clearing House, you can then put that $500 in as an itemized deduction. In other words, lottery losses can only be deducted from winnings. It doesn't seem exactly fair, but that's the way it is.

With that said, remember that I'm not an accountant, nor do I play one on TV! The best advice I can give you here is this: Save all your receipts, and then, at the end of the year, since tax laws in this country change as often as the weather, it's best for you to consult with an expert.

SHOULD I CONCENTRATE MY EFFORTS ON ONE TYPE OF CONTEST— COOKING, FOR EXAMPLE—SO THAT I BECOME AN EXPERT?

I would recommend against it, especially if you're just starting out. Although you might think you stand the best chances of winning a cooking contest, you may find that your talent really lies in writing jingles or slogans. I suggest you experiment until you see what you enjoy and what you're best at. If you want to specialize after a year or two, then go right ahead.

I READ RECENTLY THAT A NATIVE AMERICAN TRIBE IS STARTING A LOTTERY THAT MIGHT END UP HAVING THE BIGGEST PRIZES IN LOTTERY HISTORY. IS THIS TRUE?

Yes. A Native American group in the Midwest is toying with the idea of starting a national lottery that may surpass the jackpots of "Lotto America" or any of the jackpots of the largest states. As you may know, there is already a lottery run by the Oneida tribe in Wisconsin. But the new lottery, which is still in the planning stages, will be much more widespread. It's still too soon to talk about the details, but keep an eye open for it.

HOW DO I GO ABOUT STARTING MY OWN LOTTERY POOL? THERE ARE NONE NEARBY THAT I TRUST.

As I mentioned earlier, I'm a big believer in the lottery pools that are springing up across the country. They dramatically increase your odds of winning, while at the same time lowering the cost of playing. If you don't have a lottery pool near you that you like, go ahead and start your own. Here are a few guidelines:

- Make sure everybody knows the rules: How much each person will be contributing, what kind of tickets will be purchased, how often the pool will play lotteries, etc.
- Delegate assignments right away, and make sure people live up to their responsibilities. It's vital that the people who are charged with collecting the money, buying the tickets, keeping track of the tickets, and distributing Xerox copies of the tickets, perform their functions competently and diligently. If they lack the necessary skills, it would be best to replace them immediately. That

goes for members as well. If they don't ante up their share of money, make it clear to them that they will not receive their share of a win.

- Keep the membership at a manageable size. I've heard of clubs as large as 50 members, which to me seems unruly. When just starting out, I recommend keeping the pool at around 20 people. You'll accomplish your main goal, which is to increase the odds and lower the cost. And you'll also have a nice-sized group for making new friends and socializing. Most importantly, you'll avoid the logistical headaches that come from too large a pool.

- Make sure everyone agrees on the numbers to be played. If it's going to be a quick pick pool (which is my preference) then make sure everyone understands that they won't be allowed to play specific numbers. If your pool does allow numbers to be played, make sure everyone knows what they will be, and the regularity with which they'll be played.

- Approach people you trust and with whom you're comfortable. I think the best place to look is at the workplace, where pool members will be easily accessible for collection of money. You might also try a local tavern, a bowling league, or any other pre-existing group that can double as a lottery pool.

WHAT HAPPENS WHEN A VERY OLD PERSON WINS THE LOTTERY? CAN THEY GET IT IN ONE LUMP SUM?

The last time I checked, the oldest person ever to win a lottery was an 88-year-old Vermont man in 1989. His $2 million prize should keep him in clover for the next 20 years, when he reaches 108 years of age.

Obviously, an installment system like this doesn't seem fair to the elderly who probably won't be around to enjoy the bulk of their winnings. It's especially unfair to those older people who have no one to leave their newfound fortune. Most states have adopted a system in which winners have the option of choosing to receive a lump sum payment equal to what the state would have to pay for an annuity to cover the win—normally about half the face value of the grand prize. In the case of the gentleman from Vermont, this probably would have been around a million dollars, which he could enjoy to the fullest. And it doesn't cost the state an extra penny.

WHAT IS AN ANNUITY?

An annuity is an investment plan in which the customer invests a sum of money and receives a guaranteed return. The service is usually provided by an insurance company, which receives a small percentage of the interest earned by the money. The customer receives a yearly payout from the investment for however many years the customer wishes.

In terms of the lottery and large sweepstakes, the customer is the state or business that purchases an annuity to pay winners over a 20-year period. As I mentioned earlier, if states had to pay out every lottery winner in cash, the state coffers would soon run dry.

I READ THAT LOTTERIES TRY TO TAKE ADVANTAGE OF THE POOR. IS THIS TRUE?

No. While it may be true that people with little or no disposable income do play the lottery, studies indicate that their contribution is not disproportionate to the overall population. Lotteries are frowned upon by many people because, they argue, they are a "regressive" tax. In other words, lotteries are a tax by which the poor are made to pay a greater share than the rich. Again, it's probably not a good idea to pay more for tickets than you can afford to lose. But lottery officials do not set out to target or penalize those with little money.

EVERY TIME I GO TO THE STORE, IT SEEMS LIKE THERE'S A NEW SCRATCH-OFF GAME. WHY DOESN'T MY STATE JUST PICK ONE GAME AND KEEP IT?

Your state is right to keep changing the games. Because people get bored after they play a certain scratch game for too long, states have learned that the games should be rotated at regular intervals. When new games are introduced regularly, ticket sales remain high.

IS THERE A "BEST" DAY OF THE WEEK TO BUY LOTTERY TICKETS OR ENTER SWEEPSTAKES? DOES IT MATTER IF I BUY LOTTERY TICKETS EARLIER OR LATER?

It doesn't seem to matter when you buy lottery tickets, although as we've discussed, it might give you an edge with sweepstakes and contests. There are cases in which players have bought their tickets months in advance and won and cases where people barely beat the deadline and also won. Play whenever you want or whenever you have time to get to the store.

WHEN I TRAVEL, I NOTICE THAT DIFFERENT STATES SEEM TO HAVE DIFFERENT KINDS OF LOTTERIES. ONE STATE WILL HAVE A 6/54 GAME, ANOTHER WILL HAVE A 6/49 GAME. WHAT EXACTLY DOES THIS MEAN, AND HOW DOES IT HELP MY CHANCES OF WINNING?

As we discussed earlier, there are a number of different lotto games out there. They are all based, however, on picking a certain series of numbers out of a given range. The 6/54 game, for example, means that you must pick 6 numbers from 1 to 54. A sample selection for such a game might be 6-13-22-34-44-54. Just how many numbers you must choose, and the amount of numbers you have to choose from, determines the odds. Check the following chart for the odds you can expect for certain games.

Pick 5	The Odds
5/32	1 in 201,376
5/35	1 in 324,632
5/39	1 in 575,757
5/40	1 in 658,008
5/52	1 in 2,598,960

Pick 6	The Odds
6/25	1 in 177,100
6/30	1 in 593,775
6/35	1 in 1,623,160
6/36	1 in 1,947,792
6/39	1 in 3,262,623
6/42	1 in 5,245,786
6/44	1 in 7,059,052
6/46	1 in 9,366,819
6/47	1 in 10,737,573

6/49	1 in 13,983,816
6/53	1 in 22,957,480
6/54	1 in 25,827,166

Keep in mind with these odds, however, that many games give you two chances for one dollar. In the case of the 6/54 game in New York, this lowers the odds to one chance in 12,827,166. And again, although the odds sound remote, people win every day.

WHY IS IT THAT SOME STATES HAVE LOTTERIES MORE THAN ONCE A WEEK? CAN'T PEOPLE JUST WAIT A FEW DAYS?

Again, lottery commissions across the country do whatever they can possibly do to increase ticket sales. Many states now offer twice-weekly lottos as a way of "maximizing consumer interest," which is a fancy way of saying "selling more tickets." Studies show that having more than one game a week, whether it be a lotto, scratcher, or numbers game, dramatically boosts ticket sales.

HOW DOES MY STATE DETERMINE HOW BIG THE JACKPOT IS GOING TO BE THE FOLLOWING WEEK?

They seem to know in advance. It's part science, part art, and part fortune-telling. The lottery whizzes try to project upcoming jackpots by looking carefully at a number of variables, including ticket sales and the size of the current jackpot. In most states, they try to err on the conservative side, and for good reason: if they tell the public on Thursday that a jackpot is going to be $12 million on Saturday but by Saturday night it's still only $10 million, they still have to pay the winner that extra $2 million.

DO I HAVE TO TAKE MY LOTTERY PRIZE OVER 20 YEARS, OR CAN I ASK FOR IT IN ONE LUMP PAYMENT?

In almost every state that now has a lottery game, you can only receive your payment in yearly installments. The reason, as I mentioned earlier, is that your state simply cannot afford to pay the massive prizes all at once. They would have no money left from week to week to pay prizes. Instead, states usually provide the winner with an annuity which, over the course of 20 years, equals the amount of the prize. Obviously, it costs the state much less to purchase an annuity, which acquires interest as the years go by, than to fork over the entire amount of the prize.

A few states now provide the winner with one lump sum (usually half of the jackpot amount) which, if invested wisely, should equal or exceed the grand prize amount in 20 years. You do the investing, not the state. The danger, of course, is that there are no guarantees on your investment. You could end up taking a dive or blowing the entire amount on fancy dinners in Paris. The advantage is that a wise investment portfolio could, over 20 years, more than triple. You'd come out ahead. And you have the fun of doing it yourself, rather than the state doing it. Again, this is a major decision that should be made after consulting with a competent accountant or investment specialist. Unless you really know what you're doing, I'd advise you to get advice.

WILL THE LOTTERY PAY INDIVIDUAL PRIZES TO GROUP WINNERS?

While this can vary from state to state, most state lotteries allow prize money to go to a group. However, this must be specified at the time the prize is claimed. There is usually a special form for group winnings, and in California, it is called the Lottery Multiple Ownership Claim Form.

WHAT ARE THE BENEFITS OF CHOOSING THE CASH VALUE LOTTERY OPTION OVER THE ANNUAL PAYMENTS OPTION?

Most states are starting to offer both, and this question is becoming more common. The advantage of receiving the prize in a lump sum is that you get a larger amount of money immediately instead of smaller payments over time. The disadvantage is the risk that you will be more tempted to spend the prize, or that your investments will not be as sound as if you had left the care of the money in an annuity (which is the case with annual payments). Most of the disadvantages of the lump sum stem from a person having too much control of the money. Likewise, practically no control over the money (annual payments option) may not allow you to do the most with the winnings.

IS IT ILLEGAL FOR ME TO BUY WASHINGTON, DC, POWERBALL TICKETS IF I LIVE IN NORTH CAROLINA? ARE THERE ANY AGENTS SELLING POWERBALL TICKETS BY MAIL?

If you are an adult, have a dollar to part with, and make your purchase from an authorized lottery retailer, then you can buy a lottery ticket. However, you cannot transport lottery tickets across a state line for the purpose of resale. This is against the law.

I BOUGHT A POWERBALL TICKET WHILE ON VACATION IN INDIANA, AND I WON SOMETHING. CAN I CASH IN MY TICKET IN ANY OTHER STATE THAT OFFERS POWERBALL, OR MUST I CASH THE TICKET IN INDIANA?

Because Powerball is a multistate lottery, and because each of the states operate on separate computer systems, you must cash your Powerball prize in the state that the ticket was purchased. If you were playing a single state lottery in Texas, for example, and you bought the ticket at an authorized lottery retailer in El Paso, you could cash the ticket at an authorized retailer in Houston, Dallas, or San Antonio.

IS FEDERAL INCOME TAX TAKEN OUT OF YOUR YEARLY LOTTERY CHECK? HOW ABOUT STATE TAXES?

The only difference between lottery winnings and regular wages is that you don't have to work as hard to earn lottery winnings. The IRS treats income as income, and the state will withhold the amount required by the IRS. The amount you receive after taxes are taken out will vary with each individual winner, based on his or her return.

HAS ANYONE EVER BOUGHT A WINNING TICKET AND THEN NOT COLLECTED THE PRIZE?

As frustrating as it sounds, yes—on occasion even huge jackpots go unclaimed because the winner failed to show up. I've read of one $10.5 million jackpot in Michigan that went unclaimed. It's even more common that smaller prizes from scratch cards and numbers games go unclaimed. Depending on the state, the winner normally has between 6 months to a year in which to claim the prize. If the prize goes unclaimed, the winning amount is usually rolled over into other lottery games. Although sometimes this money is simply tacked onto the lotto jackpot, it's more common for the money to be spread out, either through bonus prizes or over several lotteries. The lesson to be learned from this is, of course, don't let a lottery ticket go unchecked. In the past, I've made the mistake of sticking a lottery ticket into a drawer rather than checking it right away in the next day's paper. While it's always possible to check a ticket, you should do it right away so you don't have to worry about it.

It's intriguing to think about the fate of those unclaimed tickets. Did the people throw away $10 million without knowing it? Were they criminals who had to shun the spotlight? Did they die without being able to pass on the ticket to a friend or relative? Fate can have a lousy sense of humor.

CAN THE POWERBALL WINNER DESIGNATE ADDITIONAL RECIPIENTS, SUCH AS FAMILY MEMBERS?

Prize claims are handled by each state lottery that sells the game. State prize claim rules will vary, but generally, states prefer to issue one check and withhold taxes for one person. Note, however, that some state lotteries will issue separate checks and withhold amounts for any number of persons that are sharing a prize. The question seems to suggest that a winner may decide, after winning the jackpot, to share the prize. You should be aware that to avoid the federal gift tax, the persons who are splitting the prize must have agreed to share in the purchase price of the ticket before the win. Most people are not aware of the gift tax. When a person dies, the federal government collects an estate tax (payable by the estate) on the assets of the estate. It would be an easy thing to avoid the estate tax by simply giving the property away shortly before death. To close this loophole, the federal government also assesses a gift tax payable by the person making the gift. So, if a winner decides to give half of the winnings to someone, then the winner will be charged with a gift tax on the half of the prize he or she gives away (at rates up to 55%). And the winner is still liable for the income tax on the entire prize. If you plan to split a prize, make sure you have evidence of that intention so the IRS will not tax you for making a gift. There are some minimum amounts you can give away without incurring the gift tax, but Powerball winners can afford to give gifts that can quickly reach the maximum gift tax percentage.

WHAT HAPPENS TO PRIZE MONEY IF THE WINNER DIES?

Lottery prizes and the right to receive future payments of lottery prizes are like any other property. If a winner dies before receiving all of the payments, the right to receive the payments will pass through the will (of if there is no will, then through the laws of interstate succession) to the persons or entities named by the deceased. There can be an estate tax problem with large prizes. The IRS requires the immediate payment of the federal estate tax. This tax is based on the present cash value of the entire prize, and it is likely that an estate may not have enough cash to pay the estate tax due. In this case, the Powerball game permits the estate to request the transfer of the securities held to fund the annuitized prize. The estate can then sell all or some of the securities and use the proceeds to pay off the estate tax. The amount left over can then be distributed to the heirs. Note that there are some lottery games that do limit payments "for life." This is clearly identified in game rules and advertisements and is usually the key feature of the game ("win $XXXX a week for life").

I'VE HEARD THAT MARRIED COUPLES SOMETIMES SPLIT THE WINNINGS BETWEEN THEM, SO THAT INSTEAD OF GETTING ONE CHECK A YEAR BETWEEN THEM, THEY EACH GET A CHECK. WHAT'S THE REASON FOR THIS?

I thought at first that there was some big tax benefit for married couples when they split up their winnings, but a friend who is an accountant says that this isn't really the case. My friend says that splitting the ticket means that when one of the spouses dies, the heirs would have to pay less inheritance tax on the balance due the deceased partner. Again, if you do win a big jackpot, you should get sound professional advice.

There is, of course, another good reason for splitting a winning ticket: It greatly simplifies a divorce.

I'VE HEARD THAT IT'S AGAINST THE LAW TO GIVE AWAY LOTTERY TICKETS. IS THIS TRUE?

As far as I can tell, that's incorrect. For the states I've checked, it's fine to give away tickets. As you may have noticed, many businesses will give away lottery tickets—usually scratchers—to lure in business. I've heard of an auto dealer who gave away $100 worth of instant scratch cards with the purchase of a new truck. One customer won $10,000 on the deal, which went a long way toward paying for the truck.

HAS ANYONE EVER GIVEN AWAY A WINNING LOTTERY TICKET?

Yes, it's happened on a number of occasions, usually with confusing results. You may have heard, for example, of the New York cop who, in lieu of a tip, told a waitress that he'd split the proceeds of a lottery ticket. Neither the cop nor the waitress thought it would amount to anything. But the next day, after winning a $4 million jackpot, the honest patrolman returned and made good on his pledge. It made for a great headline for the afternoon paper: "Cop gives waitress $2 million tip." But, as fairy tale-ish as it may sound, the cop's wife wasn't too pleased with his generosity. The result was a messy court battle.

In some instances, people will sign over their winning lottery tickets for a variety of less-than-honorable intentions, such as weaseling out of child support, keeping unemployment or welfare benefits, or stiffing an estranged spouse. As often as not, such plans backfire when the person who gets the ticket signed over to them decides to keep more than promised. The lesson? If the ticket belongs to you, keep it in your name and take whatever lumps come as a result. It's not worth it to mess around.

I ONLY PLAY THE LOTTERY WHEN IT GETS OVER $20 MILLION (WHY BOTHER WITH ANYTHING LESS?). CAN YOU TELL ME HOW

OFTEN THESE KINDS OF JACKPOTS OCCUR?

You wouldn't be satisfied with a lousy 10 mil? You should try to remember what J.P. Morgan (or was it Ross Perot?) said: "A million here, a million there—it adds up." The kind of prize you and I crave usually happens after several weeks without a winner. It's known in the lottery trade as a "rollover," in which the prize money rolls over to the next game. I can't tell you with any degree of certainty how often such prizes will occur, but it seems that with more and more people playing, we've seen a subsequent increase in the number of such prizes. Just keep an eye out when three or four lotteries pass without a winner. And just ignore those paltry $3 million jackpots!

Conclusion

You now have all the information you need to get started on your new hobby of winning lotteries, sweepstakes, and contests in the 21st century! The opportunities are out there, and the advances in technology are only bringing more and more opportunities each day! By now, you should also know how to protect yourself against fraud and illegitimate contests and sweepstakes and how to get in touch with other people who share your new interest.

At this point, it's all up to you. The work isn't hard, and if you find it as relaxing and therapeutic as I do, then you can't go wrong.

By now, I'm sure you've realized that you must devote a fair amount of time and effort in order to be a serious lottery, sweepstakes, or contest entrant. Hopefully, you now realize that being a winner doesn't simply hinge upon whether or not you are lucky. A winner plays the game skillfully, entering often and playing efficiently. That is why the same people seem to win contests and sweepstakes over and over again.

Although there is no way that I can guarantee you will become a winner, if you follow the suggestions I have outlined in this book, your chances of winning should improve dramatically. It's very possible that you could become the next big winner, living the life of your dreams.

But I want to remind you of something I mentioned at the beginning of this book. As long as you are enjoying the time you spend entering promotions, then you are always winning. It might take some effort to start a contest club in your town, but isn't it worth it? The new friends you make and the new skills you learn are rewards that certainly make the effort worthwhile. I cannot think of a single hobby that does not demand a fair amount of effort. So, in your quest to become a "winner," don't forget to enjoy the thrill of playing. And if you are a contest lover, then don't forget to enjoy improving your writing, cooking, or other skills.

If you only remember three things from this book, they should be: (1) follow the rules exactly; (2) enter as often as possible; and (3) have fun!

You should be proud of yourself. You're now aware of a legitimate form of income that most people simply don't understand. So the next time your friend drops a comment like, "No one ever wins those things" or "They only give prizes to people who buy something," you can set them straight. You might even want to encourage them to buy this book!

Many people are afraid to change their lives. Many people are truly scared of success, as if the newfound responsibilities outweigh the newfound rewards. Don't fall into this trap. Grab any opportunity for success that comes your way. This is true not only in the case of promotions, but for all other aspects of life as well.

Most books such as this end with the words, "Good luck!" But I won't use these words, because by now we both understand that luck is one of the least important factors in winning sweepstakes and contests. Instead, I'd like to sign off with: "Good work. You're one step closer to winning already!"